REINFORCEMENT SCHEDULES
AND MULTIOPERANT ANALYSIS

Reinforcement
Schedules
and
Multioperant
Analysis

TRAVIS THOMPSON
and
JOHN G. GRABOWSKI
University of Minnesota

New York
APPLETON-CENTURY-CROFTS
Educational Division
MEREDITH CORPORATION

73 74 75 76 77/10 9 8 7 6 5 4 3 2 1
Library of Congress Card Number: 76–182306

PRINTED IN THE UNITED STATES OF AMERICA
390–87499–X

NTENTS

Section III. SEQUENTIAL AND CONCURRENT REINFORCEMENT SCHEDULES

PREFACE

Of those variables which are important in determining the effectiveness of a given reinforcing operation, the least studied until 1957 was the specific contingency between an operant and the presentation of the maintaining consequences. Publication of Ferster and Skinner's *Schedules of Reinforcement* represents the first substantial recognition of the importance of reinforcement contingencies. *Schedules of Reinforcement* was the report of extensive and intensive research dealing with the basic simple reinforcement schedules, and some of the more complex schedules. The book functions as an encyclopedia of reinforcement schedules.

Students entering the field of operant conditioning wishing to gain familiarity with the import of reinforcement schedules have two choices: First, they may go to *Schedules of Reinforcement* and, using the book as an encyclopedia, seek out information. Alternatively, they may thumb through the cumulative index of the *Journal of the Experimental Analysis of Behavior* in an effort to find all references to a given type of reinforcement schedule. Neither approach facilitates systematic teaching or learning. There has been no single systematic introduction to and discussion of reinforcement schedules available to the student of operant conditioning. The main purpose of the present volume is to provide such a systematic coverage of this extremely important field.

A second aim of the present volume is to show that not only are simple contingencies between consequences and classes of operants important in controlling the rates and patterns of occurrence of members of those classes, but smaller operant units can be combined, under the control of reinforcement contingencies, to establish larger behavioral units. Further, such units need not be trivial, in the sense that they deal with circumscribed responses of an unnatural sort, but, as is indicated toward the end of this volume, some behavioral samples are substantial and of very practical importance.

The authors are indebted to a great many people, but probably none more than our teacher, Kenneth MacCorquodale. His stimulation initiated our interest in the subect of reinforcement schedules, and his editorial guidance has improved and made this manuscript more readable. We are clearly deeply indebted to C. B. Ferster and B. F. Skinner as well as their co-workers, who contributed to *Schedules of Reinforcement*. Similarly, this volume has been made possible to a large degree because of the body of knowledge published in the *Journal of the Experimental Analysis of Behavior* between 1958 and 1969. Readers will note the particular contribution of Jack D. Findley's work to the present volume. Not only the cooperation of the original authors of articles in permitting us to reproduce their data, often in a modified form, but also the continued assistance of the managing editor of the journal, Kay Dinsmoor, in providing us with releases for the use of their material for the present publication is gratefully acknowledged. Equal thanks goes to the students during three years of classes of Psychology 119, Analysis of Complex Behavior, at the University of Minnesota, who served as a test population for the evaluation of this program. Without their assistance the program would have a great many more weaknesses than it does. Finally, we are most appreciative of the very hard work of Judy Volinkaty and her secretarial staff in preparing the various revisions of this manuscript, and to Barbara Buraimo and Jan Carlson for their meticulous work in preparing the figures.

REINFORCEMENT SCHEDULES
AND MULTIOPERANT ANALYSIS

ALTHOUGH THIS BOOK assumes little prerequisite knowledge of psychology, a student who has had an introductory psychology course that covered the basic principles of operant conditioning will undoubtedly find the program a little easier.

Students unfamiliar with the use of programmed textbooks may need some assistance in approaching this book. The reading material is divided into small units or frames. One frame should be read and, when required, answered before proceeding to the next frame. Always check to see that you have answered correctly before proceeding. A raised dot at the end of an answer blank indicates that the answer blank is continued on the next line. A multiple-word answer is indicated by the number of answer blanks provided.

At the end of each section of the program is a set of questions summarizing the primary objectives of the section. The student should be able to answer at least 90 percent of the questions before proceeding to the next section. Any questions he is unable to answer should be looked up in the program before proceeding. Also, at the end of each section of the program will be found a list of references, with frame numbers where those references were used. In each case where original data were used in composing a frame, the original citation will be found so that the interested student or professional can look up the original article for more information.

Advanced graduate students or professionals using the program may wish to proceed directly to more advanced material rather than complete the introductory material in Section I. However, for purposes of continuity, it may be worth spending the extra time to review Section I before embarking on the remainder of the program. The review questions at the end of each section provide the opportunity to evaluate the necessity of studying a given section.

Section I

INTRODUCTION

I-1

This is an introduction to reinforcement schedules and analysis of multioperant behavior repertoires. /

I-2

The occurrence of present behavior is largely controlled by the *consequences* of past behavior. This program deals exclusively with behavior whose future occurrence is controlled by the _____ of current actions of the environment. /

consequences

I-3

Behavior whose future occurrence is controlled by the _____ of a current action on the environment is called *operant behavior.* /

consequences

I-4

The defining properties of an *operant,* a specified case of _____ behavior, are (1) the response class, (2) the stimulus conditions prior to reinforcement, (3) the contingencies for reinforcement, and (4) the nature of reinforcement. /

operant

I-5

The (1) response class, (2) the stimulus conditions prior to reinforcement, (3) the contingencies for reinforcement, and (4) nature of reinforcement are the defining properties which comprise the basic unit of analysis called a(n) _____. /

operant

3

An action on the environment, called a *response,* may have as its consequence a stimulus change, which is called a *reinforcing event,* or *reinforcement.* /

Responses leading to a specified reinforcing event or _____ may vary considerably in topography (e.g., form, pattern, force) from one *response instance* to another. /

reinforcement
  (not reinforcer since
  that is a stimulus rather
  than an event)

Since the topography of responses leading to reinforcement may vary, we refer to a specific case of the action on the environment as a(n) _____ instance, while the general family of actions on the environment is called a(n) _____ class. /

response
response

We might respond to a person one morning by saying "Hi," and on another morning by saying "Hello." A specific occurrence, on a given morning, of the greeting "Hello" is an example of a response _____●
_____. The general category of "morning greeting behavior" is an example of a response _____. /

instance
class

The defining properties of a(n) _____ are (1) a general family of reinforced behaviors called a(n) _____ _____, (2)

4

the stimulus conditions prior to reinforcement, (3) the contingencies for reinforcement, and (4) the nature of reinforcement. /

operant
response class

I-11

There are two general categories of response class. In one case the reinforcing event, or reinforcement, is dependent on the emission of a response. Such a(n) _____ instance is a member of a *positive* _____ *class*. /

response
response

I-12

When reinforcement is dependent upon the emission of a response of a given class, the response is a member of a(n) _____ *response class*. /

positive

I-13

When reinforcement is dependent on the *nonemission* of a response of a given class, the response is a member of a negative _____ _____● _____. /

response class

I-14

Thus, the two general categories of response class are the _____ _____ _____, in which reinforcement is dependent on the emission of a response of a given class, and the _____ _____ _____, in which reinforcement is dependent upon the nonemission of a response of a given class. /

5

positive response class
negative response class

In some job situations, emission of large amounts of work is reinforced by the employer, while nonemission of work is socially reinforced by fellow employees. The former circumstance defines a(n) _____ •
_____ response class, while the latter defines a(n) _____ response class. /

positive
negative

I-16

An important aspect of negative _____ is that they always involve *temporal contingencies*. /

operants

I-17

A teacher tells the children in her class that if everyone is quiet for 15 minutes they can all go out and play. The teacher has specified a(n) _____ reinforcement contingency, which is a necessary feature of a negative operant. /

temporal

I-18

In a positive response class, (emission, nonemission) of a response leads to reinforcement; in a negative response class, (emission, nonemission) of the response leads to reinforcement. /

emission
nonemission

I-19

As a defining property of an operant the response class specifies the behavior required to obtain the reinforcer. A second defining property of an operant, the *stimulus conditions prior to reinforcement*, can be manipulated to specify periods during which a response will be reinforced or will go unreinforced. /

Manipulation of the stimulus conditions prior to reinforcement can consist of presenting a stimulus (e.g., a light or tone), during which instances of a given response class will be reinforced. /

A stimulus which is presented and during which instances of a given response class are reinforced is called a *discriminative stimulus* (S^D). That is, a stimulus which indicates availability of reinforcement dependent on instances of responses of a given class is called a(n) _____ _____. /

discriminative stimulus

A discriminative stimulus indicates that instances of a given response class will be _____. /

reinforced

Manipulation of stimulus conditions prior to reinforcement can consist of presentation of a discriminative stimulus which indicates availability of reinforcement. However, stimuli can also be presented which indicate nonavailability of reinforcement. Such a stimulus is called an *S-delta* (S^Δ). /

An S-delta is a stimulus which indicates _____ _____ of reinforcement and during which instances of a given response class go _____● _____. /

nonavailability
unreinforced

7

A stimulus indicating nonavailability of reinforcement and during which instances of a given response class go unreinforced is called a(n) _____. /

S-delta (or S△)

Two stimulus categories can be involved in stimulus conditions prior to reinforcement. Presentation of stimuli of one category indicates availability of reinforcement for instances of a given response class. Stimuli of this category are called _____ _____. Presentation of stimuli of a second category indicates nonavailability of reinforcement for instances of a given response class. Stimuli of this category are called _____. /

discriminative stimuli
S-deltas

There are several ways in which response class and stimulus manipulations can be combined. For example, one response class can be specified and one stimulus may be periodically presented which indicates availability of reinforcement only during this stimulus [i.e., a(n) _____ _____]. /

discriminative stimulus

If one stimulus is presented which indicates availability of reinforcement for instances of a given response class, only during this stimulus, such a stimulus is a(n) _____ _____. Since reinforcement is only available during the presence of this stimulus, the absence of this stimulus serves as a(n)   (discriminative stimulus,   S-delta). /

discriminative stimulus
S-delta

8

In the preceding situation reinforcement was available in the presence of a stimulus and period of non-availability was indicated by the absence of the stimulus. Another way to accomplish alternation of stimulus conditions indicating availability and non-availability of reinforcement would be to use _____ (number) stimuli. /

two

In this situation one stimulus could be presented which specified (availability, nonavailability) of reinforcement, thereby serving as a(n) _____ _____, while the other could specify (availability, nonavailability) of reinforcement and serve as a(n) _____. /

availability, discriminative
 stimulus
nonavailability, S-Delta
(either order)

In the preceding example presentation of one stimulus indicated reinforcement availability while the other stimulus indicated nonavailability of reinforcement for instances of a given response class. Since only one response class is specified, there are periods during which reinforcement is available and periods during which it is not available. /

The use of two response classes and two stimuli establishes a situation in which instances of one response class (e.g., lever press) can be reinforced in the presence of one stimulus (e.g., red light) and not reinforced in the presence of the second stimulus (e.g., green light), while instances of the other response class (e.g., chain pull) can be reinforced in the presence of the second stimulus (green light) but

9

not in the presence of the other stimulus (red light). /

I-33

If lever presses are reinforced in the presence of a red light but not in the presence of a green light, the red light is a(n) _____ _____ while the green light is a(n) _____. /

discriminative stimulus
S-delta

I-34

If chain pulls are reinforced in the presence of a green light but not in the presence of a red light, the green light is a(n) _____ _____ while the red light is a(n) _____. /

discriminative stimulus
S-delta

I-35

The preceding example describes a situation using two response classes and two stimuli. During one stimulus, reinforcement was available for instances of one response class but not for the other, while during the second stimulus reinforcement was available for instances of the other response class but not for instances of the first response class. Therefore, one stimulus functions as a discriminative stimulus for one response class and a(n) _____ for the other response class. The second stimulus functions as a(n) _____ _____ for the second response class and a(n) _____● _____ for the first. /

S-delta
discriminative stimulus
S-delta

I-36

Since one response class is reinforced in the presence of one stimulus and not in the presence of the second stimulus and the second response class is reinforced in the presence of the second stimulus but not in the presence of the other stimulus, each stimulus is serving two functions. That is, both stimuli are serving as _____ and _____. /

discriminative stimuli
S-deltas
(either order)

I-37

The preceding example describes a situation using two response classes and two stimuli. It is clear that while the defining property of an operant called a response class specifies the behavior _____ to obtain reinforcement, the stimulus conditions prior to reinforcement (a second defining property) may be manipulated to specify the availability or _____● _____ of reinforcement for instances of a given response class. /

required
nonavailability

I-38

The presence or absence of a specified stimulus or the presence of the stimulus may serve different functions for different response classes. /

I-39

Providing a stimulus which is intended to serve as a discriminative stimulus or as an S-delta will not necessarily have an effect on behavior. When a stimulus is provided and behavior covaries with its presence or absence, the stimulus is said to exert *stimulus control* and the behavior is said to be under _____ *control*. /

stimulus

I-40

The presentation of a stimulus which indicates the

11

availability of reinforcement and during which instances of a given response class are reinforced is serving a discriminative function only if the behavior covaries with its presence or absence. In this case presentation of the stimulus (should, should not) be followed by instances of the response class if the behavior is under _____ _____●
_____. /

should

stimulus control

I-41

When a stimulus is presented which indicates the nonavailability of reinforcement and during which instances of a given response class go unreinforced, the stimulus is serving an S-delta function only if the behavior covaries with its presence or absence. In this case presentation of the stimulus (should, should not) be followed by instances of the response class if the behavior is under _____ _____●
_____. /

should not

stimulus control

I-42

Manipulation of the stimulus conditions prior to reinforcement can specify when responses will be reinforced. Covariation of the behavior with the stimulus conditions indicates that stimulus control has been established. This is an important feature in the analysis of operant behavior. /

I-43

In the preceding frames we have frequently referred to the *reinforcing* event or reinforcement, an important variable in the development and maintenance of operant behavior. *Reinforcement* is the occurrence of a consequence of a specified operant. /

I-44

A reinforcing event or _____ must occur in a specified temporal relation to an operant. /

reinforcement

I-45

When an operant is followed by _____, there is an increased probability of the recurrence of that operant. /

reinforcement

I-46

The probability of the recurrence of a given operant increases when _____ is dependent, or as we refer to it, *contingent,* on the occurrence of that operant. /

reinforcement

I-47

If reinforcement is dependent, or _____ on the occurrence of an operant, it is said that a *contingency for reinforcement* exists. /

contingent

I-48

In considering contingencies for reinforcement we note that they specify the existence of a specific co-variation between the occurrence of an operant and its controlling consequence, or _____. /

reinforcement

I-49

Thus, the covariation between water running out of a faucet and turning the handle of a faucet specifies the contingencies _____ _____. /

for reinforcement

13

The existence of a specific _____ between the occurrence of a response of a given class
and reinforcement denotes the existence of contingencies for reinforcement. /

covariation

Thus, another of the defining properties of an operant
is the _____ for reinforcement. /

contingency

The defining properties of an operant are (1) the ____●
_____ class, (2) the stimulus conditions
prior to reinforcement, (3) the _____
for reinforcement, and (4) the nature of reinforcement. /

response
contingencies

When it is stated that reinforcement is contingent on
the occurrence of a response of a given class, the
term "reinforcement" specifies the event (a reinforcing event) but does not specify the stimulus (a reinforcing stimulus). /

A reinforcing event which is contingent on the occurrence of a response of a given class is referred to as
_____; the stimulus itself is referred to as
a *reinforcer* or _____ *stimulus*. /

reinforcement
reinforcing

14

The occurrence of a specific stimulus following the occurrence of a response of a given class can be considered a reinforcing _____, or _____● _____, only if its occurrence increases the probability that the response which it follows will recur. /

stimulus
reinforcer

A stimulus following a response can be considered to be a reinforcer or _____ stimulus only if its occurrence increases the _____ that responses of that class will recur. /

reinforcing
probability or *frequency*

We find that under certain conditions (e.g., not having eaten for 2 days) food is an effective reinforcer for most humans. Responses leading to food will increase in _____. /

probability or *frequency*

Humans traditionally categorized as "anorexics" do not emit responses which have food as a consequence. Therefore, the presentation of food upon the emission of a response cannot be termed _____● _____; and the food itself is not a(n) _____ stimulus or reinforcer, since it does not increase the _____ that responses of that class will recur. /

reinforcement
reinforcing
probability or *frequency*

15

An "anorexic" for whom reading is a high probability response may emit eating behavior if the opportunity to read is made contingent on eating behavior. In this case presentation of the opportunity to read is termed _____, and reading books is a reinforcer if there is an increase in the probability of "_____ behavior." /

reinforcement
eating

Reinforcers which are effective without prior *conditioning* are called *unconditioned* _____. /

reinforcers

There are two types of reinforcers which are effective without prior conditioning, that is, are _____ *reinforcers.* /

unconditioned

A stimulus whose presentation following the occurrence of an operant increases the probability of recurrence of members of that class without prior conditioning is called an *unconditioned positive* _____. /

reinforcer

Water is an example of a stimulus whose presentation usually increases the probability of the operant which it follows. Thus, water is a(n) _____ _____. /

I-64

The emission of a member of a class of responses leading to an unconditioned positive reinforcing event is a positive operant. /

I-65

Since the above case involves the emission of a response of a given class and the presentation of a reinforcer, it illustrates a case of a(n) _____ operant followed by _____ _____● _____ reinforcement. /

positive
unconditioned positive

I-66

In another type of operant, the presentation of water would be contingent on the non_____ of a response of a given class. We would then be dealing with a(n) _____ operant. /

(non)*emission* or
  occurrence
negative

I-67

A stimulus whose withdrawal or removal, following the occurrence of an operant, increases the probability of recurrence of members of that class without prior conditioning is called a(n) *unconditioned negative* _____. /

reinforcer

I-68

Electric shock is an example of a stimulus whose removal may increase the probability of the operant which its removal follows. Thus, electric shock is a(n) _____ _____ _____● _____. /

I-69

The emission of a member of a class of responses leading to an unconditioned negative reinforcing event, in which electric shock is the reinforcer, is a positive operant. /

I-70

The above case involves the emission of a response of a given class and the withdrawal of a reinforcer; it illustrates a case of a (positive, negative) operant that involves _____ _____ reinforcement. /

positive

unconditioned negative

I-71

In another type of operant, the removal of electric shock would be contingent on the non_____ of a response of a given class. We would then be dealing with a(n) _____ operant. /

(non)emission

negative

I-72

While unconditioned reinforcers are effective as reinforcers without prior conditioning, other stimuli, which are ineffective or only weak reinforcers, may acquire substantial reinforcing properties through repeated presentation in close temporal contiguity with an unconditioned reinforcer. Such stimuli are called *secondary* or *conditioned* _____. /

reinforcers

I-73

An unconditioned reinforcer may be referred to as

a primary _____. Another name for a
conditioned reinforcer is _____ _____●
_____. /

reinforcer
secondary reinforcer

I-74

When the presentation of a reinforcer increases the
probability of recurrence of the operant which it follows, it is a positive _____. When the
withdrawal of a reinforcer increases the probability of
the recurrence of the operant it follows, it is a negative _____. /

reinforcer
reinforcer

I-75

When the *presentation* of a conditioned reinforcer
strengthens the response it follows, it can appropriately be called a *conditioned* _____
reinforcer. /

positive

I-76

The click of the food magazine in an operant-conditioning test chamber can reinforce a response it follows. The click is a(n) _____ _____●
_____ reinforcer. /

conditioned positive

I-77

A conditioned reinforcer whose removal following
the occurrence of a member of a given response class
strengthens that class is called a conditioned _____●
_____ reinforcer. /

negative

19

The termination of a tone which has repeatedly been paired with shock will strengthen a response leading to tone termination. The tone is a(n) _____ _____ reinforcer. /

conditioned negative

Under certain conditions, the opportunity for an organism to emit a response leading to reinforcement may be removed. For example, the subject may be removed from the experimental situation, or the lever may be removed from the test chamber. A period during which the opportunity to emit a reinforced response is removed is called a *time out* and is abbreviated _____. /

TO

At other times the contingencies of reinforcement are changed independent of the organism's behavior. Such situations are called *behavior independent events* and are abbreviated _____. /

BIE

When food is present noncontingently, we say that a behavior independent event has occurred. /

Having considered the BIE, we now see that generally the relation between the organism's behavior and reinforcement is limited to three categories: (1) The emission of specified behavior produces certain consequences (_____ operants); (2) the nonemission of specified behavior produces certain consequences (_____ operants); (3) the environmental events or consequences occur independently of behavior (referred to as _____ _____). /

positive
negative
behavior independent
  events

The type of reinforcing event (e.g., positive or negative, conditioned or unconditioned) was described as
one aspect of the nature of reinforcement, which is
one of the defining properties of a(n) _____.
The other aspect of this property involves the stimulus
conditions and contingencies which follow reinforcement of a given response instance. /

operant

The type of reinforcing event conditioned or _____●
_____, positive or _____,
and subsequent stimulus conditions and contingencies
for reinforcement are the two aspects of the defining
property referred to as the nature of _____. /

unconditioned
negative
reinforcement

The defining properties of an operant are (1) the response _____, (2) the stimulus condi-
tions prior to reinforcement, (3) the _____
for reinforcement, and (4) the nature of _____●
_____. /

class
contingencies
reinforcement

The initial rate of occurrence of an operant prior to
conditioning is its *operant level*. /

21

Repeated reinforcement of an operant increases the frequency of occurrence of the response class above the _____ _____. This process is called *operant conditioning.* /

operant level

When behavior has been strengthened by the process of _____ _____, it is said to be *conditioned.* /

operant conditioning

When, through reinforcement, a response class has been _____, repeated occurrence of the responses of the specified class without reinforcement will result in a decrease in its strength. This process, involving withholding of _____, is called *operant extinction.* /

conditioned

reinforcement

The repeated occurrence of a previously reinforced operant, which is no longer reinforced, results in a diminution of the strength of the operant. This process is called operant _____. /

extinction

Response rate is one of the most sensitive measures of the extent to which various factors (e.g., contingencies for reinforcement) control _____ behavior. *Response* _____ is particularly useful since it may serve as an independent variable as well as a dependent variable. /

operant
rate

I-92

The basic datum used to determine the strength of a response of a given class is response _____. /

rate

I-93

Response rate is said to be an expression of response probability or _____ strength. /

response

I-94

Thus, the primary dependent variable in operant-conditioning research is _____ _____●
_____. We will discuss in a later portion of this program how _____ _____●
_____ may also be manipulated as an independent variable. /

response rate
response rate

I-95

A convenient way of recording operant behavior which provides immediate access to response rate is a *cumulative record* of the organism's responses. /

I-96

Commercially manufactured *cumulative recorders* are used to directly record the subject's behavior. Such recorders have two basic parts: (1) a constant-rate paper feed which drives the paper from a roll inside the recorder over a drum, and (2) a response-step pen, which writes from the bottom to the top of the paper, moving by fixed increments as each response is made. The response-step pen is also capable of making another mark, a diagonal slash, which usually indicates the presentation of a reinforcer. /

Illustrated in the figure is a *cumulative recorder* (I) and a portion of a *cumulative record*. The mechanism that provides constant-rate paper feed is at *A* and the pen is at *B*. II and III are enlarged sections of the cumulative record. III-1 shows the distance of pen travel upon the occurrence of a response. III-2 shows the distance of pen travel between two responses in this particular case (the distance represents the *interresponse time*, which we will discuss later). At III-3 is a diagonal slash indicating reinforcement, and at III-4 is a second diagonal slash, which is followed by the return of the pen to the other edge of the paper. (It is said that the pen "resets.") /

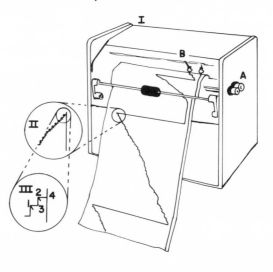

III shows the last _____ (number) responses before the pen "_____." At I-1 there is a diagonal movement of the pen which indicates a(n) _____, just as the diagonal line seen at II-1. /

3

resets

reinforcement

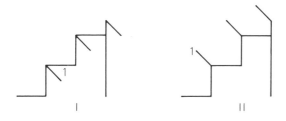

I   II

In the preceding example of a cumulative record we see that the abscissa (horizontal axis) indicates _____ _____, while the ordinate (vertical axis) indicates the number of _____. /

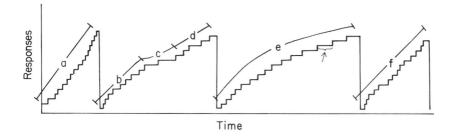

Time

---

time

responses

I-100

In the section of the record designated by a there is a medium slope which indicates a moderate _____● _____ of responding. /

rate

I-101

The slopes at *b* and *c* are less than the slopes at *a*. This indicates that the rate of responding has (increased, decreased). /

decreased

25

I-102

From c to *d* in the figure the curve is slightly positively accelerated. In section e, however, the curve is ________________ accelerated. Section e thus indicates a progressively (increasing, decreasing) rate of responding. /

negatively
decreasing

I-103

At times we find periods of zero rate of responding, such as at the arrow in e. /

I-104

Though the slopes at *a* and __ are quite similar, the pattern of responding is quite different. /

f

I-105

One result of recording the number of responses over time is that slopes of various degrees are produced. Comparison of ________________ yields a relative measure of ongoing operant behavior. /

slopes

I-106

Cumulative response records provide immediate visual access to response rate by the ________________ of the record. The steeper the slope, the (higher, lower) the response rate. /

slope
higher

I-107

A cumulative record of operant behavior, such as the one shown here, indicates a(n) (diminishing, increasing) response rate and is (positively, negatively) accelerated. /

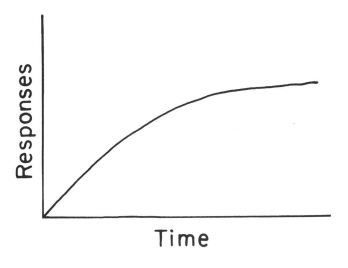

Responses

Time

---

diminishing
negatively

I-108

Draw a curve which indicates a progressively increasing response rate. This curve is _____ accelerated. /

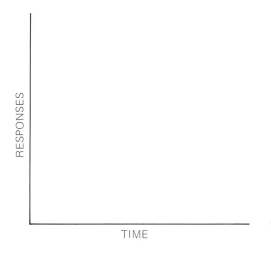

RESPONSES

TIME

positively

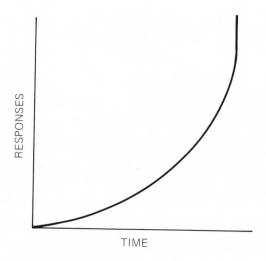

Examine the cumulative record shown here. During period *A*, responses were recorded but not reinforced. During period *B*, each response was reinforced. During *C*, reinforcement was discontinued. /

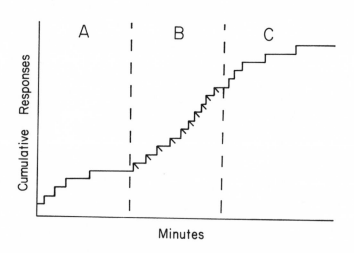

28

I-110

In *A* the _____ level was determined. /

operant

I-111

The process of diminishing response rate illustrated during the *B* period is called operant _____. /

conditioning

I-112

The process of diminishing response rate illustrated during the C period is called operant _____. /

extinction

I-113

The rate of responding for a relatively long period (e.g., minutes or hours) without regard for details of performance within that interval is called the *overall rate*. /

I-114

Within an experimental period with a given overall _____, response rate may vary from moment to moment. Such momentary rates within a session are called *local rates*. /

rate

I-115

Within a given session with a specified overall rate, it is possible to specify a *mean rate* for portions of the session (e.g., from the first to the 50th reinforcement), although within this portion local _____ changes may exist. /

rate

Thus, overall rate usually refers to a (larger, smaller) portion of a session than does mean rate. /

larger

And local rate refers to (larger, smaller) portions of an experimental session than does mean rate. /

smaller

In the cumulative record shown, the _____ rate was approximately 10 responses per minute, while the _____ rate oscillated from approximately 20 responses per minute to a zero rate. /

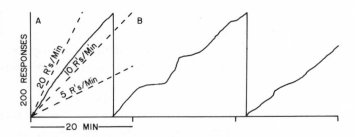

overall
local

For the 1-hour session illustrated the performance during A indicates a high _____ rate. /

local

The _____ rate during B is lower than the _____ rate during A. /

30

overall
local

I-121

When responses occur in clusters with more-or-less regularly distributed patterns of intervals between such clusters, variable local rates prevail. /

I-122

Clusters of responses which are widely distributed produce a cumulative record which may be character- ized as having variable _____ _____●
_____. /

local rate

I-123

Clustering is determined by the lengths of time be- tween successive responses. The time elapsed be- tween successive operant responses is called the *inter-response time* and is abbreviated _____●
_____. /

IRT

I-124

The _____ is the elapsed time between initiation of the response $(R—1)$ and the next response (R). This _____ _____
is a measurable property of the response (R_n). /

IRT
inter-response time

I-125

A frequency distribution of inter-response times is called a(n) _____ *frequency* _____●
_____. /

IRT (frequency)
  distribution

Thus, by recording the time between 11 successive responses it is possible to plot a(n) _____ distribution, with 10 different inter-response times. /

IRT

Consider the following 10 inter-response times (from response N—1 to response N):

$$\begin{array}{l} 1 \text{ to } \ 2 = 1 \text{ second} \\ 2 \text{ to } \ 3 = 5 \text{ seconds} \\ 3 \text{ to } \ 4 = 3 \text{ seconds} \\ 4 \text{ to } \ 5 = 2 \text{ seconds} \\ 5 \text{ to } \ 6 = 4 \text{ seconds} \\ 6 \text{ to } \ 7 = 3 \text{ seconds} \\ 7 \text{ to } \ 8 = 4 \text{ seconds} \\ 8 \text{ to } \ 9 = 6 \text{ seconds} \\ 9 \text{ to } 10 = 3 \text{ seconds} \\ 10 \text{ to } 11 = 2 \text{ seconds} \ / \end{array}$$

If these 10 IRTs are plotted, the distribution shown is obtained. From examining the IRT distribution it is apparent that the greatest number of inter-response times were spaced _____ seconds apart. /

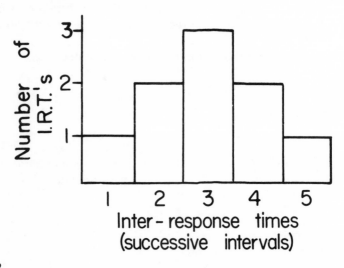

32

I-129

IRT distributions are seldom nearly symmetrical as in the preceding case. Consider the case shown here. The least frequent inter-response time was _____ _____ seconds. In fact, the greatest numbers of responses seem to be spaced _____ second and _____ seconds apart, with relatively few responses spaced 2 to 4 seconds apart. /

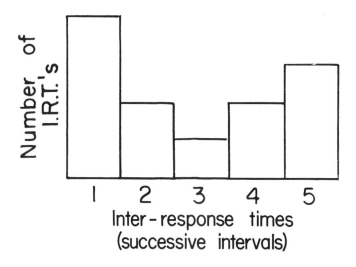

I-130

As the peak (mode) of an IRT distribution shifts to the left, there are relatively (fewer, more) short IRTs. /

more

I-131

Compare the two IRT distributions shown. /

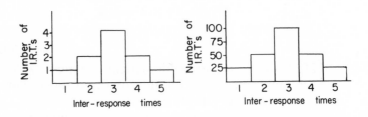

Notice that the shapes of the IRT distributions are identical, but the number of IRTs plotted differ by a factor of 25. These distributions could result from unequal time periods or from the use of different IRT bin durations (i.e., different time units on the abscissa). In either case response rate is not necessarily reflected in the shape of the IRT distribution. /

Since IRT distributions cannot be used to compare *absolute* response rates, they are usually plotted in terms of _____ frequency of various inter-response times. /

relative

If one wishes to determine the pattern of intervals between successive responses, for periods of unequal lengths or where absolute overall rates differ, it is the usual practice to express the IRT distribution in terms of _____ _____. /

relative frequency

However, even correcting for differences in absolute rates by expressing IRT distributions in terms of relative frequency does not eliminate all the difficulties. There is a bias favoring occurrence of many short IRTs because every opportunity for a longer IRT necessarily means that an opportunity for shorter IRTs preceded it. /

Thus, in the preceding case, for an IRT of 5 seconds to be recorded, IRTs of 1, 2, 3, and 4 had to be possible first. Since there was no response during the last four intervals, they can be viewed as IRT opportunities, and the frequency of occurrence of responses at various IRTs can be expressed as number of *IRTs per opportunity.* /

If the data in Frame I-127 are reconsidered, we see that there were a total of 10 inter-response times, or IRT _____.

IRT	Responses	Opportunities	IRTs/Opportunity
1	1	10	0.10
2	2	9	0.22
3	3	7	0.43
4	2	4	0.50
5	1	2	0.50
6	1	1	1.00

For IRTs of 1 second, all 10 opportunities occurred. For IRTs of 2 seconds, all opportunities were available except shorter IRTs (i.e., 1 second). Thus, there were 9 opportunities. Similarly, for IRTs of 3 seconds, all equal or longer IRTs provided opportunities; thus there were _____ opportunities. /

opportunities
seven

The distribution of IRTs per opportunity shown here summarizes these data. It can be seen that instead of a symmetrical distribution, a positively accelerated function results, with the most IRTs per opportunity occurring at _____ seconds. /

6

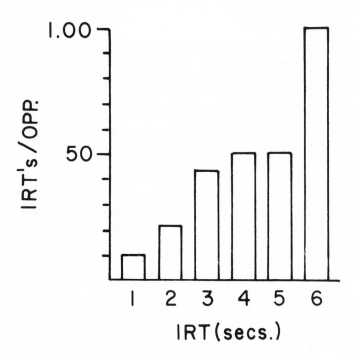

In other words, when a correction is made for the bias favoring short IRTs we find the mode of the IRT distribution shifting to long IRTs. /

Thus, the distribution of inter-response times corrected for differences in absolute numbers of responses expressed as _____ frequency of IRTs, and corrected for bias favoring short IRTs, expressed as IRTs per _____, can yield information not obtainable from response rate measures. /

relative
opportunity

36

Objectives

1 What are the four defining properties of an operant?
I-4 to I-61

2 What are the distinguishing features of a response class and a response instance?
I-7 to I-9

3 What are the two categories of response class?
I-11 to I-18

4 What are the two types of operants and what is the necessary feature of negative operants?
I-15 to I-18

5 What are the two general categories of stimuli which may be presented in relation to a given response class and reinforcement and what does each indicate?
I-19 to I-42

6 Aside from reinforcing properties, what functions may a stimulus serve?
I-30 to I-36

7 How is covariation between stimuli and behavior related to the concept of stimulus control?
I-39 to I-42

8 Are reinforcement and reinforcer synonymous terms? Explain.
I-7, I-43, I-53 to I-55

9 What is the relationship described by a contingency of reinforcement?
I-46 to I-51

10 What is the necessary effect on occurrences of responses of a given class if a stimulus is a reinforcer?
I-45 and I-46

11 What are the distinguishing properties of the two types of conditioned and unconditioned reinforcers?
I-60 to I-78

12 How does a conditioned reinforcer acquire reinforcing properties?
I-72 to I-78

13 What is the definition of time out?
I-79

14 What is a BIE and how does it differ from "standard" contingencies for reinforcement?
I-79 to I-81, I-46 to I-51

15 What are the three possible and all-inclusive types of contingencies which relate behavior to its consequences?
I-82, I-15, I-16 to I-18, I-79 to I-81

16 To what does the term "operant level" refer?
I-86 to I-87

17 What is the term referring to the process through which reinforcement of responses of a given class increases its frequency?
I-87

18 What is operant extinction?
I-89 to I-90

19 What is the basic datum used to determine the strength of a given response class?
I-91 to I-93

20 The cumulative recorder provides a record of responses as a function of what variable? Is this a measure of rate?
I-97 to I-105

21 A cumulative record gives a direct measure of time and total number of responses. What feature of the record gives overall response rate?
I-100 to I-105

22 How would you interpret a cumulative record where the response line was parallel to the ordinate (i.e., zero slope)?
I-102 and I-103

23 Describe "negative acceleration" in terms of response rate.
I-107 and I-108

24 If extinction is complete, what is the response rate and what is the appearance of the cumulative record?
I-109

25 To what do the terms "overall rate," "mean rate," and "local rate" refer? How are they related in terms of the size of the "unit" to which they refer?
I-113 to I-222

26 How is an IRT measured?
I-123 to I-126

27 What aspect of response rate in time does an IRT distribution express?
I-123 to I-135

28 An IRT distribution does not necessarily reflect response rate. Why not?
I-132

29 Of what is IRT/OPP a measure and why might it be used?
I-136 to I-140

References

Anger, Douglas, "The Dependence of Inter-response Times upon the Relative Reinforcement of Different Inter-response Times." *Journal of Experimental Psychology, 52,* No. 3 (Sept., 1956), 145–161.

SIMPLE
REINFORCEMENT
SCHEDULES

II-1

In Section I, the defining properties of the operant were stated as (1) the response class, (2) the contingencies for reinforcement, (3) the stimulus conditions prior to reinforcement, and (4) the nature of reinforcement. /

II-2

The present section considers *simple reinforcement schedules*. A schedule is specified in terms of contingencies for reinforcement. A contingency for reinforcement exists when the occurrence of a reinforcing event is _____ on the occurrence of a response of a given class. /

contingent

II-3

The conditions under which a response of a given class is reinforced are the _____ for _____; these contingencies define the *reinforcement schedule*. /

contingencies
reinforcement

II-4

The contingencies for reinforcement specify the conditions under which a response will be reinforced and therefore define the _____ ____•
_____. /

reinforcement schedule

II-5

All _____ _____ may be defined in terms of *temporal* (e.g., elapsed time between possible magazine operations) and/or *response* (e.g., number of switch operations) requirements. /

reinforcement schedules

II-6

When a reinforcement schedule is defined only in terms of _____ (e.g., elapsed time) and/or _____ (e.g., switch operations) requirements, it provides a purely formal statement of the reinforcement schedule. /

temporal
response

II-7

A reinforcement schedule defined in terms of _____● _____ and/or _____ re-quirements, without reference to behavior generated, provides a purely _____ _____ of the contingencies for reinforcement. /

temporal
response
formal statement

II-8

The formal statement of a reinforcement schedule is a description of procedures for initiating and terminating stimuli in relation to temporal and/or response requirements, and is made without reference to _____ generated by the controlling contingencies. /

behavior

Reinforcement schedules may also be described in terms of behavior _____ by the controlling contingencies, in which case we refer to *"characteristic performance"* generated by a specific set of contingencies. /

generated

II-10

The description of a reinforcement schedule in terms of the behaviors generated by the controlling contingencies is based on the fact that a given schedule results in a *characteristic* _____. /

performance

II-11

A given schedule of reinforcement may be defined without reference to behavior as a(n) _____ _____ of temporal and/or response requirements. /

formal statement

II-12

Alternatively, a reinforcement schedule may be characterized in terms of the behavior generated by the controlling contingencies, that is, in terms of the___● _____ _____. /

characteristic
 performance

II-13

A third way in which reinforcement schedules may be defined is in terms of general principles controlling features of behavior generated by specific contingencies (e.g., probability of reinforcement, or reinforcement frequency). /

42

When defining a reinforcement schedule in terms of reinforcement frequency, it is described by *general* _____. /

principles

Description of a schedule in terms of temporal and/ or response requirements without reference to be- havior generated involves a purely _____ _____. /

formal statement

Description of a schedule in terms of an organism's behavior involves specification of the _____ _____ generated by the contingencies. /

characteristic performance

Description of a schedule in terms of probability of reinforcement involves characterization by a(n) _____● _____   _____. /

general principle

Prior to instating the contingencies for reinforcement and subsequent conditioning, the rate of occurrence of the *operant* is determined; that is, we determine the _____ *level.* /

operant

Technically, only when it is known that an organism has no past history of reinforcement involving a

given operant is it proper to refer to the rate of occurrence prior to conditioning as the _____
_____. /

operant level

II-20

Most behaviors emitted by human adults have been,
or are presently, under the control of some *reinforcement schedules*. When dealing with previously conditioned behaviors, their rate of occurrence prior to
contingency manipulation is called the *baseline* rate
rather than _____ _____. /

operant level

II-21

The rate of occurrence of an established operant
prior to the onset of contingency manipulation is
called the _____ rate. /

baseline

II-22

With human and infrahuman subjects, response rate
associated with the *characteristic performance* on a
given reinforcement schedule on which the effects of
experimental manipulations are to be evaluated (e.g.,
schedule change or stimulus change) is called the __●
_____ _____. /

baseline rate

II-23

While the operant level is a baseline rate, not all
baseline rates are operant levels. /

II-24

In the absence of a relevant *past reinforcement history*, the rate of occurrence of a response of a given
class prior to conditioning is called the _____
_____ _____; the rate

44

of occurrence of an operant prior to contingency manipulations is referred to as the _____ rate. /

operant level
baseline

The primary difference between operant level and the baseline rate is in regard to the organism's _____● _____ _____ of _____● _____. /

past history
reinforcement

The determination of operant level is followed by instating the _____ that specify a given _____ _____. /

contingencies
reinforcement schedule

NONINTERMITTENT REINFORCEMENT SCHEDULES

II-27

Frequently researchers using operant techniques with infrahumans *develop* the operant with a reinforcement schedule in which the only reinforcement contingency is the occurrence of a single response (e.g., lever press). This is called a *regular* or *continuous reinforcement schedule*, abbreviated CRF. /

II-28

When the contingencies for reinforcement are such that the only specified requirement for reinforcement is the emission of one response of a given class, the contingent relation is called _____ *reinforcement*, abbreviated _____. /

continuous

CRF

II-29

Since all responses have the same consequences (each response is reinforced) on a(n) _____ schedule of reinforcement, it is referred to as a *non-intermittent* reinforcement schedule. /

continuous

II-30

A CRF schedule is one of two schedules which are referred to as _____. A continuous reinforcement schedule specifies that each response occurrence will be _____. /

nonintermittent
reinforced

II-31

While each occurrence of the operant is reinforced on a(n) _____ (abbreviation) schedule, an *extinction* schedule, abbreviated *EXT*, specifies that no responses will be reinforced (i.e., all responses go _____). /

CRF
unreinforced

II-32

A reinforcement schedule specifying that all responses go unreinforced is called a(n) _____ schedule, abbreviated _____. /

extinction
EXT

II-33

Two reinforcement schedules which specify that the

46

consequences of each response are the same are
_____ (abbreviation) (each response is
reinforced) and _____ (abbreviation)
(each response goes unreinforced); both are _____●
_____ schedules of reinforcement. /

CRF
EXT
nonintermittent

II-34

The contingencies specifying that no responses will
be reinforced [i.e., a(n) _____ sched-
ule] are instated *after conditioning* and thus after a
history of reinforcement. This case of responses going
unreinforced is quite different from the determination
of the rate *prior to conditioning* (i.e., _____
_____). /

extinction
operant level

II-35

Animals which have not previously been reinforced
in an operant-conditioning chamber may emit responses incompatible with lever pressing when first
placed in the apparatus. The decrease in frequency
of these behaviors is referred to as *adaptation*. /

II-36

After a short time in an operant-conditioning apparatus, responses incompatible with lever pressing decrease in frequency. This is referred to as, but not
explained by, the term _____. /

adaptation

II-37

Following placement in the apparatus and *adaptation* of incompatible behaviors the *operant level* of
the specified response class is determined. /

This stylized figure shows the general appearance of a cumulative record of an animal's performance without a past history of reinforcement in the apparatus. The record follows the period of *adaptation*. Since no contingencies were in effect between a and b, response occurrences were not _____.
This portion of the record represents the determination of the _____ _____
of responding. /

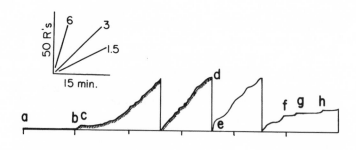

reinforced
operant level

Following b, the contingencies in effect specified that each response occurrence would be reinforced. Instatement of the CRF schedule cannot have an effect on the lever-pressing rate until a(n) _____ occurs. /

response

Between c and d the stable and intermediate rate usually generated by a(n) _____ (abbreviation) schedule is apparent. /

CRF

48

The brief period of high rate at e is referred to as "bursting" and is a characteristic effect of withdrawal of a positive reinforcer. In this case, food was no longer being presented upon response emission. Therefore, a(n) _____ schedule was in effect. /

extinction

The initial (low, high) rate resulting from instating an extinction schedule is followed by several alternations between high and low rates from e to f. The general curvature of the record between these two points exhibits _____ acceleration. /

high
negative

Between f and g no responses are emitted; there is a pause in responding, followed by a brief period of responding and another _____. After h no further responses were emitted; it is said that the operant has undergone _____. /

pause
extinction

The occurrence of the characteristic period of high rate upon instatement of an extinction schedule is referred to as "bursting." It is generally considered an aggressive behavior pattern elicited by withdrawal of the opportunity to obtain reinforcement. /

Adaptation of incompatible responses occurs when an animal is first placed in the apparatus. This term is also used to refer to the decrease in bursting when an extinction schedule is reinstated after reconditioning. /

When the term "adaptation" is used in reference to the decrease in "bursting" upon reinstatement of an extinction schedule, it refers to a decrease in an elicited _____ behavior pattern resulting from withdrawal of the opportunity to obtain _____. /

aggressive
reinforcement

If reinstatement of the continuous reinforcement schedule is followed by reinstatement of an extinction schedule, (more, less) aggressive behavior, which is seen as "bursting," may be expected. Again this is referred to as, but not explained by, the term _____●
_____. /

less
adaptation

A is an example of a cumulative record generated by a young girl's maladaptive behavior (vomiting under the contingencies of an extinction schedule) after an extensive history on a continuous reinforcement schedule (not shown). Removal from the classroom and return to the dormitory had been the reinforcing consequence of this behavior. When the response class of this operant was no longer _____, the rate _____. (At *B*, draw a record of the performance as it would appear when under the control of a CRF schedule.) /

reinforced
decreased

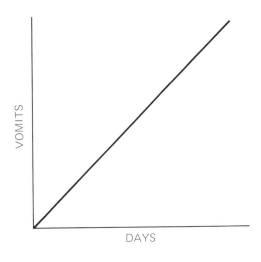

VOMITS

DAYS

II-49

A reinforcement schedule which specifies that each occurrence of the operant will have the same conse-quence (e.g., CRF and EXT) is referred to as a _____●
_____ reinforcement schedule, while schedules which do not specify the same conse-quence for each response instance are referred to as *intermittent* reinforcement schedules. /

nonintermittent

II-50

CRF, a *nonintermittent* reinforcement schedule, is useful for the establishment of behavior; contingen-cies specified by *intermittent* reinforcement schedules are more useful for the maintenance of behavior. /

II-51

To this point we have considered two _____ schedules (CRF and EXT). Now we will consider schedules in which not every response instance is reinforced. These are referred to as _____ reinforcement schedules. /

51

nonintermittent

intermittent

INTERMITTENT
REINFORCEMENT SCHEDULES

Fixed Ratio
Reinforcement Schedules

II-52

In a *fixed ratio* schedule of reinforcement, abbreviated FR, the occurrence of the response is reinforced on completion of a fixed number of responses counted from the preceding reinforcement. /

II-53

Reinforcement schedules in which reinforcement occurs upon the completion of a fixed number of responses counted from the preceding reinforcement are called _____ _____ schedules, abbreviated _____. /

fixed ratio

FR

II-54

In a *fixed ratio* reinforcement schedule every *n*th response occurrence produces a reinforcing stimulus (thus, the consequences are *not* the same for each occurrence of the response). Therefore, a(n) _____●
_____ _____ schedule (unlike CRF) is a(n) _____ reinforcement schedule (except FR 1, which is identical to CRF). /

fixed ratio

intermittent

52

In fixed ratio schedules, reinforcement is contingent upon a(n) _____ number of _____● _____ emissions. /

fixed

response

The word "ratio" refers to the ratio of responses to reinforcement. This is given as a number after the letters FR (e.g., _____ 10). /

FR

Instatement of a new schedule (e.g., FR) produces an immediate change in contingencies but does not result in an immediate shift to performance characteristic of the new schedule. /

The period following instatement of a new schedule, but prior to development of characteristic performance, is called *transition* (e.g., *transition* from characteristic performance under a CRF schedule to performance characteristic under a FR schedule, or simply _____ from CRF to FR). /

transition

When a new schedule is instated, the performance is initially a function of the characteristic performance developed under the preceding schedule (i.e., part of the past history of reinforcement) and the contingencies of the new schedule. /

The period during which the contingencies for reinforcement are those of a new schedule, while the
behavior is to some extent under the control of the
contingencies of both the _____ and
_____ schedule, is referred to as ____●
_____ . /

old (and) *new*
(either order)
transition

The figure is a stylized plot of the transition from CRF
to FR. The performance is determined by both the
old and new schedules, although the contingencies
are those of the FR schedule. /

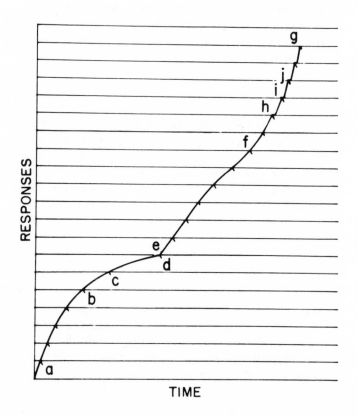

TIME

This stylized record illustrating the _____ from CRF to FR shows a high but decreasing rate between a and b, and a very low rate between c and ___. The initial effects of instating a fixed ratio schedule are quite similar to those resulting from instatement of a(n) _____ schedule after CRF. /

transition
d
extinction

FR contingencies come into effect during the decrease in rate, especially between c and d. Since reinforcement is contingent upon the emission of a fixed number of _____, low rates result in long inter-reinforcement times, while high rates produce more frequent reinforcement. /

responses

Under the contingencies of an FR schedule, low rates, as found between c and d, result in long inter-reinforcement times, while high rates, as seen at e, produce (more, less) frequent reinforcement. /

more

The stylized plot illustrates slight negative acceleration (as it did between a and b) between e and ___, followed by _____ acceleration between ___ and g. /

f

positive

f

"Pausing" after reinforcement (which frequently occurs on fixed ratio schedules) is evident at __, __, and __. This is referred to as *post-reinforcement pause*. The term "post-reinforcement pause" is descriptive of the temporal locus of the characteristic pause. However, recent studies strongly suggest that the stimuli correlated with the upcoming ratio actually control the post-reinforcement pause. (The relevant data will be discussed in Chapter 3.) /

h

i

j

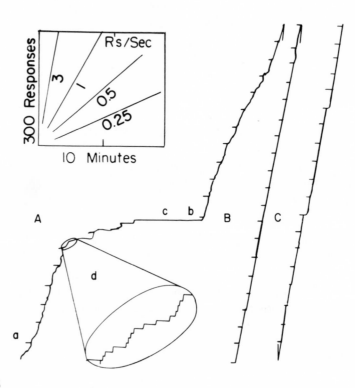

II-68

The cumulative record shown illustrates performance by a pigeon on a key pecking operant. Segment *A* is the ________________ from CRF to FR 40. Segments *B* and *C* illustrate characteristic performance and good schedule control. /

transition

II-69

The initial effect of instating the FR schedule (the portion of the record between *a* and *b*) was similar to instatement of a(n) ________________ schedule after CRF. This negatively accelerated portion ends with a long ________________ at c. /

extinction

pause

II-70

At *d* is an enlarged portion of the segment illustrating local rate variability in the pattern of responding. /

II-71

In segments *B* and *C* a sustained high rate (approximately ________________ responses /sec) is apparent. /

3

II-72

Final performance (segment *C*) includes several ratios with positive acceleration to terminal rate following longer ________________ pauses. /

post-reinforcement

In general, the transition from CRF to small FR schedules is characterized by (1) (low, high) but decreasing
rates [similar to the effects of instating a(n) _____●
_____ schedule], (2) alternation be-
tween positively and _____ accelerated
curves, and (3) local rate _____. /

high
extinction
negatively
variability

The characteristic performance on small FR schedules
includes (1) _____ rates, (2) brief _____
_____ after reinforcement, and (3) occasionally slight positive acceleration after the pause
at the beginning of the ratio. /

high
pauses

The terms "small," "intermediate," and "large" applied to the value of ratio schedules must be considered in terms of the organism. While FR 22 was
considered a "short" fixed ratio for pigeons, FR 5
might be termed "small" and FR 11 "large" when the
subject is a 10-year-old gelding, as is apparent in the
record shown on the opposite page. /

Characteristic performance is exhibited by this retired
workhorse (nudging a lever with its nose) under fixed-
ratio schedules of reinforcement. /

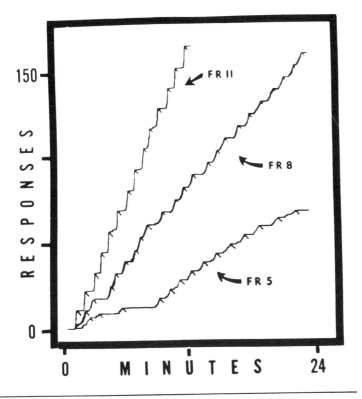

RESPONSES

150 —

0 —

0   M I N U T E S   24

FR 11

FR 8

FR 5

The _____ after reinforcement may be explainable by the fact that the animal required 30 seconds to consume the food reinforcer. In later records of pigeons' performances, long "pauses" after reinforcement will be illustrated which are consistently longer than the time required to consume a food reinforcer. /

pauses

II-78

As stated earlier, "large" or "small" as applied to ratio size are relative terms and such factors as species and the nature of the operant must be considered. /

II-79

The cumulative record segment at A is from a session after an extended history of reinforcement on FR 60. The response rate is (less, greater) than 2 responses/ sec. /

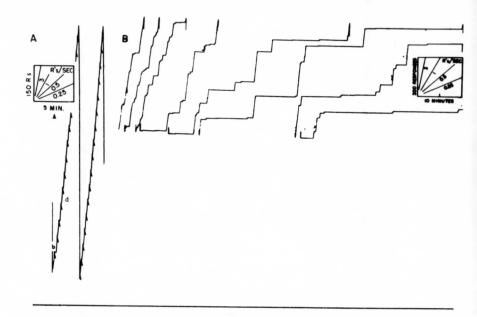

II-80

B in the figure is a record of a single session of performance under an extinction schedule after an extended history of reinforcement on FR 60. The rates are generally in excess of 5 responses/sec. This record (*B*) is characterized by (high rates, low rates, high rates and pauses)./

high rates and pauses

II-81

In comparing the pause duration, we find that pauses early in the session are (shorter, longer), while those later in the session are (shorter, longer)./

shorter
longer

II-82

Comparison of the *pauses* and *runs* of responses early and late in the session shows that runs of responses early in the session are (shorter, longer), while those later in the session are (shorter, longer). /

longer
shorter

II-83

In general, performance under an extinction schedule after an extended history of reinforcement on a fixed ratio schedule is characterized by (1) _____ rates of responding (comparable to performance under the fixed-ratio contingencies), and (2) progressively _____ pauses. /

high
longer

II-84

Records of performance after a brief period on a fixed ratio schedule are similar. Although fewer responses are emitted in extinction, the general pattern of ____● _____ rate responding and progressively _____ pauses is predictable. /

high
longer

II-85

The pattern of runs and pauses will be similar regardless of the length of the past history of reinforcement, while generally the number of responses emitted under an extinction schedule will be (greater, the same, fewer) after an extended or brief history of reinforcement. /

greater

II-86

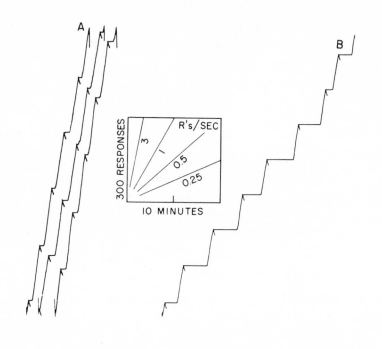

In the figure, A is a record of characteristic performance on an FR 200 (relatively large ratio) and B is a
record of characteristic performance on an FR 120
(intermediate ratio)./

The *overall rate* in A is approximately _____
responses/sec, while in B it is approximately (3, 1,
0.25) responses/sec./

3

1

While the overall rate is greater in record A, the local
rate in record A is (greater than, the same as, less
than) the local rate in B./

the same as

II-90

While in record *B* there is an abrupt local rate change from zero to the maximum rate, in *A* there is slight _____ acceleration to the terminal rate. /

positive

II-91

It is important to note that the local running or maximum rate of an organism at two different FR values may be the same, and that the difference in overall rate is frequently due to differences in the length of the _____ pause. /

post-reinforcement

II-92

Whether a decrease in overall rate occurs on larger ratios is dependent on the relative increase in the size of the fixed ratio (larger ratios provide fewer opportunities for post-reinforcement pause) in comparison to the increase in length of the post-reinforcement pause. /

Irregularities on Fixed Ratio Reinforcement Schedules

II-93

Irregularities in performance may appear under fixed ratio schedules which are apparent in the resultant records. Specifiable sources include (1) abrupt large increase in the fixed ratio, (2) insufficient reinforcement, and (3) sudden introduction of novel stimuli. /

II-94

In general, all but the very smallest increases in the ratio will initially result in an increase in the length of the _____ after reinforcement. This performance is generally transient, and only brief pauses appear as stable performance develops. /

63

II-95

Large increases in the fixed ratio frequently result in continued local _____ variability and extended and irregular _____ after reinforcement. /

rate
pauses

II-96

A less frequent irregularity involves an initial run of responses after reinforcement, followed by negative acceleration and a pause, and then completion of the ratio. The appearance of such a sequence in the record is called a *knee*. /

II-97

Continued irregularities in performance due to large increases in the ratio include (1) *local rate* _____●_____, (2) _____ and irregular pauses after reinforcement, and (3) _____● _____ (a "run" at the terminal rate, followed by negative acceleration and a pause, then completion of the ratio). /

variability
extended
knees

II-98

This record of a pigeon's performance on an FR 125 illustrates two of the irregularities discussed. Variability in the pause after reinforcement is seen in comparing the pauses at *a*, *b*, and *d*, while a marked _____ is seen at c. /

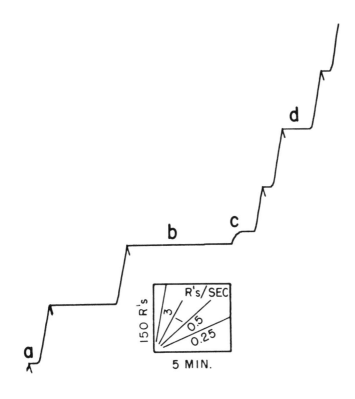

R's/SEC

150 R's

3

0.5

0.25

5 MIN.

---

knee

The performance resulting in records showing knees is characterized by (1) a run of responses at a high rate followed by (2) _____ acceleration and a (3) pause, and then (4) _____ of the ratio. /

negative
completion

Irregularities in pausing and a "knee" appear in the record due to large increases in the size of the fixed ratio. If stable performance has been exhibited at a lower ratio, we would expect that the irregularities could be eliminated and stable fixed ratio performance achieved by (increasing the ratio, continuing the present ratio, decreasing the ratio). /

decreasing the ratio

A *1* illustrates a bird's performance on an FR 180. Irregularities are evident in the post-reinforcement pauses. /

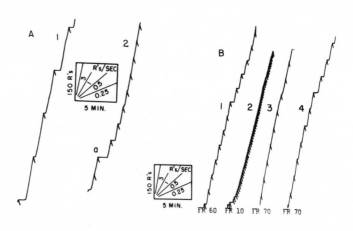

Segment *2* of *A* shows the effects of a *decrease* in the ratio to FR 65. Reduction of the ratio does not immediately eliminate all pausing, as can be seen at *a*. /

The performance is under an FR 60 schedule in segment *B 1*, which exhibits irregularities in *post-*_____●
_____ *pause*. /

reinforcement

The fixed ratio was reduced from an FR 60 to an FR 10 in segment *B 2*. The pauses are rapidly eliminated. /

66

The transition to the lower ratio at *B 2* is quite similar to segment *A 2.* /

Reduction in the size of the fixed ratio, in general, (does, does not) immediately reduce the length of the post-reinforcement pause. /

does not
(although not immediate,
the change does occur
quite rapidly)

In *B 3* the ratio was increased to FR 70. *B 4* shows that the increase was too large for the maintenance of stable performance, as evidenced by the post-reinforcement pauses and overall _____ acceleration. /

negative

Irregularities in performance under fixed ratio schedules may result from increases in the ratio. The irregularities which appear in the records after such increases include (1) variable _____ rate, (2) irregular _____ pauses, and (3) _____. Irregularities in performance under fixed ratio (and other) schedules may also result from insufficient reinforcer magnitude. /

local
post-reinforcement
knees

In the record shown are the initial segments of sessions 2 through 6 on an FR 20 schedule when a magazine malfunction reduced the amount of reinforcement after each ratio completion. The resultant records illustrate FR 20 performance under conditions of insufficient reinforcer magnitude or insufficient _____. /

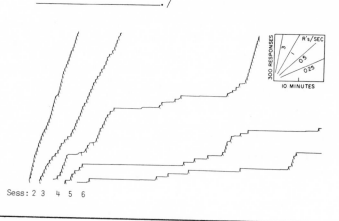

Sess: 2 3   4   5   6

reinforcement

There is a progressive decrease in _____ rate in segments 2 through 6, owing to an increase in the number and length of the _____. /

overall

pauses

Although there are deviations in local rate, in general a (low, high) running rate is maintained. /

high

The primary effect of insufficient reinforcement on this smaller ratio has been a lengthening of the ____ _____ _____. /

post-reinforcement pause

In the record shown we see a decrease in the overall

rate and maintenance of the running rate, while in the record presented in this frame (insufficient reinforcement on FR 50), there is a(n) _____ in the overall rate and a(n) _____ in the running rate. /

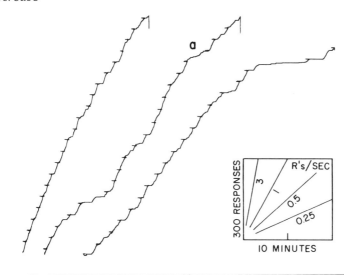

II-114

Also apparent is variable local rate as at _____. However, the pauses after reinforcement do not change greatly. The curve is quite (similar to, different from) one in which a ratio which is too high has produced similar decline in overall rate. /

II-115

Therefore, either insufficient reinforcer magnitude or inadequate frequency of reinforcement may result in failure to maintain characteristic performance. Irregularities resulting from either of these sources are said to be due to _____ _____. /

II-116

Thus far we have seen that either a(n) _____●
_____ in the ratio size and/or conditions of _____   _____
tend to have extremely disruptive effects on schedule
control. A third source from which irregular performance may result is *novel stimuli.* /

increase

insufficient reinforcement

II-117

The record shown (A) illustrates the performance
(following 5000 reinforcements on FR 50) resulting
from a change in the key light to a novel color at the
beginning of this session. /

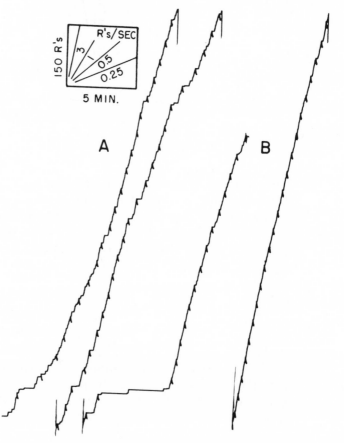

II-118

The occurrence of the key color change (a(n) _____●
_____ *stimulus*) has characteristic
effects on performance, most notably a decreased
rate of emission of most behaviors. /

novel

II-119

Pauses are evident and variable local rate appears.
Two sessions later (segments in *B*) the record indicates an approximation of more characteristic FR performance. /

II-120

A(n) _____ stimulus may generate
variability in local rates and lead to an overall decrease in the rate of occurrence of other behaviors. /

novel

II-121

Three specifiable sources producing irregularities in
performance on fixed ratio schedules of reinforcement include a (1) _____ _____●
_____ in the size of the fixed ratio, (2)
conditions of _____ _____,
and (3) _____ _____. /

large increase
insufficient reinforcement
novel stimuli

II-122

Earlier we found that schedule control could be re-
gained if a ratio had been increased too rapidly by
_____ the size of the ratio. Additional
control can be gained by means of an *added stimulus*. /

decreasing

II-123

A stimulus, some dimension of which is designed to remain proportional to some feature of a schedule of reinforcement (or performance generated by that schedule) is referred to as an *added* _____. /

stimulus

II-124

Under the contingencies of a fixed ratio schedule, the most important feature involves the number of _____ required for reinforcement. Therefore, the added stimulus utilized is one which changes proportionally in relation to the number of responses emitted; it is referred to as a(n) _____●
_____ counter. /

responses
added

II-125

The added stimulus on a fixed ratio reinforcement schedule is referred to as a(n) _____
_____. It provides more effective control of behavior and is readily manipulable by the investigator. /

added counter

II-126

The form of added counter used with pigeons is a slit of light on the response key which increases in length as a function of the number of responses completed in the ratio. The result is more effective *control* of *behavior* than that generated by the _____●
_____ alone. /

schedule

1 in the figure illustrates the progression of the added counter in the form used in a pigeon's response key. 2 simply shows the slit at its smallest and largest dimensions. /

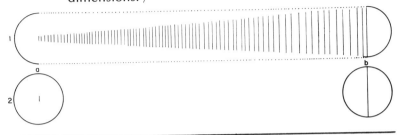

A record of performance on a fixed ratio schedule with an added counter is shown. The light slit began to lengthen as a function of the number of responses at a (i.e., operation of the external stimulus as a(n) _____   _____). /

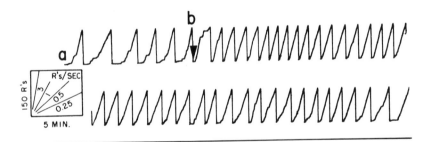

added counter

The effect of the operation of the added counter at a is not unexpected since we learned earlier that disruption of performance may result from the occurrence of _____   _____. /

novel stimuli

The disruptive effects of the "added counter," which

is initially a novel stimulus, include a decrease in the rate to zero at *a*. /

Between *a* and *b*, the atypical performance of the bird is apparent as irregularities in the record. Comparison of local rates in the portion between *a* and *b* shows a reduction in the irregularities over successive ratio completions. /

Following *b* the added counter was reversed. When the original counter was in effect, the slit size _____ _____ as a function of the number of responses. Therefore, it was smallest at the beginning of the ratio and _____ at the end. After the reversal, the slit size decreases as a function of the number of responses. Therefore, it is smallest at the end of the ratio and _____ at the beginning. /

increased
largest
largest

If the rate under the original counter was low at the beginning of the ratio and the behavior was under control of the added counter, when the counter is reversed the slit size at the end of the ratio will be (large, small) and the rate will be _____. /

small
low

If the rate at the end of the ratio was high under the original counter, the rate at the beginning of the ratio under the new counter should be _____, provided the behavior is under *stimulus* _____● _____. /

II-135

Analysis of the record at the first ratio after reversal shows that the large slit after reinforcement controls (high, low) rates as it did immediately (after, prior to) reinforcement under the original counter. /

high
prior to

II-136

Further examination of the first ratio after the reversal shows that the small slit controls (high, low) rates as it did (after, prior to) reinforcement under the original counter. /

low
after

II-137

In general, the ratio performances prior to reversal of the counter are (directly, inversely) comparable to ratio performance following the reversal. (_____●
_____ acceleration is evident before reversal; _____ acceleration is evident after reversal.) /

inversely
positive
negative

II-138

In this case the combination of the added stimulus and the bird's behavior has (marked, no) effect on overall rate. /

no

II-139

The new counter begins to take effect in the second portion of the record and the performance drifts to

that more typical of _____ _____●
_____ schedules. /

fixed ratio

When stimulus control (hence characteristic fixed ratio performance) with the reversed counter is re-established, a second reversal (restoration of the original counter) will have predictable effects (not shown). /

II-141

The initial effects of the second reversal should be exhibited as elimination of the _____ _____ and _____ acceleration to reinforcement. /

post-reinforcement pause
negative

II-142

Initially, after the second reversal the ratio runs will be negatively accelerated, but as behavior again comes under stimulus control, the ratio runs will become _____ _____ and characteristic performance will again be evident. /

positively accelerated

II-143

This record illustrates performance under an FR 190 + counter followed by a transition to an FR 360 + counter. In this case the counter was adjusted (at the arrow) so that maximum size would be reached upon completion of the new larger ratio. /

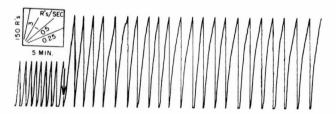

76

With the exception of a slight increase in _____●
_____   _____ (curva-
ture), the performance under the two ratios is quite
similar. /

negative acceleration

The transition to the FR 360 is relatively smooth and
irregularities such as increase in the length of _____
_____   _____ and pauses
in the middle of the ratio run do not occur. /

post-reinforcement pause

An irregularity (in terms of characteristic fixed ratio
performance) which is present, however, is _____●
_____   _____ (curva-
ture). /

negative acceleration

However, the major effect of the added stimulus is
maintenance of responding despite large increases in
the ratio. /

Objectives

1 What is the relationship between contingencies for reinforcement and a schedule of reinforcement?
II-2 to II-4
2 All reinforcement schedules may be described in terms of
what two types of requirements?
II-5 and II-6
3 What is included in a purely formal statement of a reinforcement schedule?
II-6 to II-8, II-11, II-15
4 What constitutes a description of a reinforcement schedule
in terms of "characteristic performance"?
II-13 and II-14, II-17

5 How may a reinforcement schedule be defined in terms of general principles?
II-9 and II-10

6 What differentiates between operant level and baseline rate?
II-18 to II-26

7 What are the two nonintermittent schedules discussed and what feature do they have in common? How are they different?
II-27 to II-34, II-49 to II-51

8 What term is used to describe the decrease in behaviors incompatible with the specified response class and when is it relevant?
II-35 to II-37, II-45 to II-47

9 Describe the general features of the beginning of an experiment using an operant-conditioning apparatus and the appearance of the cumulative record during operant level.
II-35 to II-47

10 What is an intermittent schedule of reinforcement?
II-51

11 What is a fixed ratio schedule (definition) and what is the abbreviated notation?
II-52 to II-56

12 Discuss the general nature of performance and controlling variables during transitions and the specific nature of CRF to FR transition.
II-57 to II-60, II-61 to II-66, II-68 to II-73

13 What is the nature of characteristic performance on FR schedules?
II-74

14 What is the characteristic rate under FR schedules?
II-73 and II-74

15 What is "post-reinforcement pause"?
II-66, II-73, II-74

16 What is the relation between runs of responses and pauses when an extinction schedule is instated following characteristic FR performance?
II-80 to II-85

17 Comparison of performance under intermediate and large FRs shows that while running rates may be equal, the overall rates may differ. Why?
II-87 to II-92

18 What are three readily specifiable sources of performance

irregularities on FR schedules?
II-93
19 What performance irregularities may occur following large increases in FR size?
II-97 to II-108
20 What are the effects of insufficient reinforcement on FR performance?
II-109 to II-115
21 What are the effects on FR performance of introduction of a novel stimulus?
II-116 to II-120
22 How may an added stimulus be used in conjunction with FR schedules and what is the effect on, and relation to, behavior?
II-123 to II-131, II-143 to II-147
23 What is the effect on FR performance of an added counter reversal?
II-132 to II-142

Variable Ratio Reinforcement Schedules

II-148

In a *variable ratio* (VR) reinforcement schedule a response is reinforced after a specified number of occurrences, the number varying from reinforcement to reinforcement. /

II-149

Reinforcement schedules in which reinforcement occurs on the completion of a given number of responses, the number varying from reinforcement to reinforcement, are called _____ _____● _____ schedules, abbreviated _____● _____ . /

variable ratio
VR

II-150

Under a VR schedule of reinforcement, the number of response occurrences required for reinforcement varies from reinforcement to reinforcement (thus, the consequences are *not* the same for each occurrence of the response). Therefore, a VR schedule (like FR, unlike CRF) is a(n) _____ reinforcement schedule. /

intermittent

II-151

In VR schedules, the number of occurrences of the response on which reinforcement is contingent varies from reinforcement to reinforcement. /

II-152

The result of using VR requirements is that there is *no* consistent, *fixed* correlation between the number of responses and the occurrence of a reinforcing event; and it is therefore less probable that behavior will come under strong control of behaviorally generated stimuli. /

II-153

Since variable ratio or _____ (abbreviation) schedules reduce the extent to which behavior can come under the control of stimuli resulting from the _____ itself, the characteristic performance generated by such schedules is unlikely to exhibit phenomena comparable to consistent post-reinforcement pauses, found under fixed ratio contingencies. /

VR
behavior

II-154

It is less probable that behavior will come under the control of _____ generated _____●_____ when the response requirements vary randomly from reinforcement to reinforcement as they do on VR schedules. /

behaviorally
stimuli

In VR and other simple schedules in which reinforcement is contingent on the number of responses, (high, low) rate is characteristic since (high, low) rate results in reduced frequency of reinforcement. /

high
low

II-156

More frequent reinforcement occurs under VR schedules when response rates are _____; low rates result in _____ frequency of reinforcement under VR schedules. /

high
reduced

II-157

Under VR schedules, as under fixed ratio schedules, high rates produce reinforcements (less, more) frequently. /

more

*Specification of Variable Ratio
Reinforcement Schedules*

II-158

Following specification of the *mean ratio size* and the *smallest* (usually 1) and *largest ratios,* an *arithmetic* or *geometric* progression is usually used to determine the ratio values. /

II-159

The average, or mean, ratio size and the extreme values of the ratios [i.e., the _____ (usually 1) and _____ ratios] are the general specification of a VR schedule. /

smallest
largest

The ratio values between the extremes are most commonly evolved through the use of a(n) _____●
_____ or _____ progression. /

arithmetic
geometric

The mean ratio size is arbitrarily selected, with the knowledge that excessive increases in response requirements will result in (cessation, high rate) of responding. /

cessation

The numbers between the smallest ratio and the largest ratio would be derived from an arithmetic progression if they were (1, 11, 21, 31, 41, 51 or 2, 4, 8, 16, 32, 64). The mean ratio in this case would be approximately (29, 26, 21, 15). /

1, 11, 21, 31, 41, 51
26

An important aspect of specification of the ratios is that of *step size*. Although a VR schedule consisting of 1, 11, 21, 31, 41, 51 and a VR schedule of 1, 26, 51 have the same extreme values and _____
ratio size, very different performance will result due to the difference in step _____. /

mean
size

When specifying the contingencies in the design of a VR schedule, we must include (1) the size of the mean _____, (2) the values of the ___●

_____ and _____ ratios,
and (3) the values between the extremes and step __●
_____. /

ratio
smallest (and) *largest*
size

II-165

Following specification of the mean ratio, extreme
values, step size, and ratio values between the extremes, the ratio values are randomized, thereby
making the requirements unpredictable at any moment, and therefore reducing the extent to which
performance is under the control of _____
generated stimuli. /

behaviorally

II-166

When referring to a given fixed ratio schedule we
used the abbreviation followed by a number which
indicated the ratio size (e.g., FR 40). Since the ratio
size changes from reinforcement to reinforcement
under a(n) _____ _____
schedule, refer to a given schedule of this type using
the abbreviation and the size of the mean ratio. /

variable ratio

II-167

A VR schedule with a mean ratio of 26 would be
written as _____ _____. /

VR 26

II-168

Shown is a stylized curve of transition from CRF to
VR. The horizontal lines represent reinforcements;
they occur after varying distances on the vertical axis,
which represents _____. /

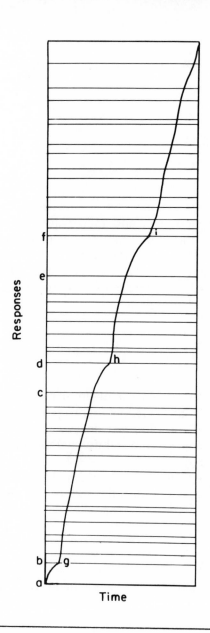

Responses

Time

responses

The initial rate (between a and b) is higher than that which was generated by the preceding CRF schedule (not shown). The (high, low) rates following removal

of the CRF contingencies is referred to as _____●
_____. /

high
bursting

II-170

The high rate which follows removal of the CRF schedule has been attributed to aggressive behavior. High rate is reinforced just after _____, and therefore maintained. /

b

II-171

The stylized curve illustrates (between c and d) what may occur if a slightly larger ratio is programmed among the smaller ratios; _____ acceleration appears, as it does when an extinction schedule is instated. /

negative

II-172

The effects of another occurrence of a larger ratio are illustrated between _____ and _____●
_____. /

e (and) f

II-173

The overall rate under VR schedules is illustrated in the stylized curve as being _____, although intermediate rates do occur. /

high

II-174

Following reinforcement, a frequent occurrence under VR schedules is a rate (decrease, increase) as seen at _____, _____, and _____. /

increase
g, h, (and) *i*

The primary features of performance generated by VR schedules illustrated above are the (low, high) overall rate and rate (decrease, increase) following reinforcement. /

high
increase

A is a record of transition from CRF to an arithmetic VR 40 schedule. The high rate of responding after CRF results in a high frequency of _____. /

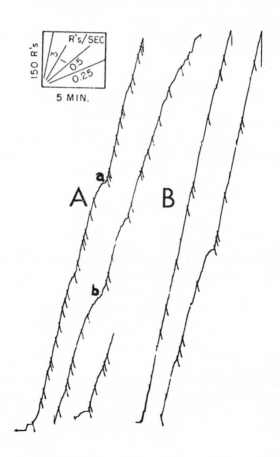

reinforcement

At *a* and *b*, larger ratios result in performance which appears as _____ _____ (curvature) in the record. /

negative acceleration

Unlike the performance generated by FR schedules, the VR schedule does not result in consistent _____ _____ pause. /

post-reinforcement

In the segments in *B* we see that the mean ratio size has been (increased, decreased). Although irregularities are present, the overall rate is (low, high). /

increased
high

Performance generated by fixed ratio schedules may include _____ after reinforcement. At *a*, *b*, and *c* it is evident that performance generated by variable ratio schedules may include (decreased, increased) rate following reinforcement. /

pauses (or *pausing*)
increased

Examination of the record of performance prior to reinforcement at *a*, *b*, and *c* indicates (decreasing, increasing) rate; the higher rate after reinforcement is followed by an abrupt or gradual change to (lower, higher) rate. /

decreasing
lower

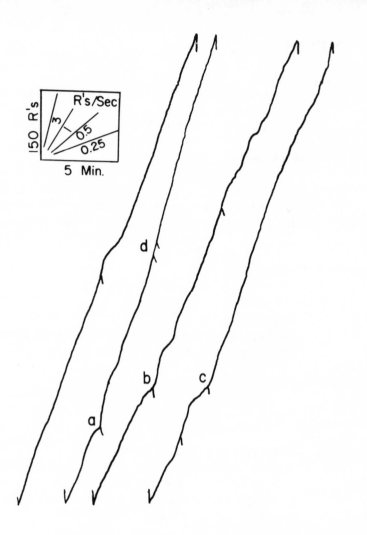

The decreasing rate prior to *a, b,* and *c* occurred during relatively (short, long) ratios, and the decreased rate following the period of high rate occurs during relatively (short, long) ratios. /

long
long

At *d* a short ratio results in reinforcement during the period of high rate after the preceding reinforcement, and the rate (decreases, is maintained). /

is maintained

If during the period of high rate following reinforcement another reinforcement occurs, (decreased, maintenance of high) rate might be expected; if another reinforcement does not occur during the period of high rate, (decreased, maintenance of high) rate might be expected. /

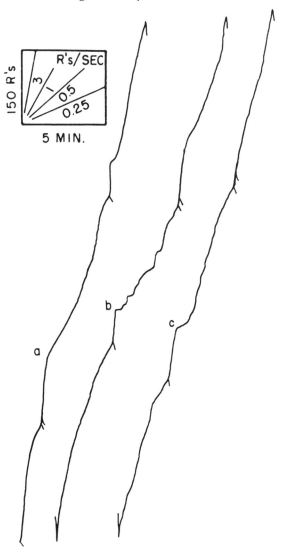

maintenance of high
decreased

II-185

The figure is a portion of a record generated under a VR 360 schedule four sessions after the record shown in Frame II-180. /

II-186

In this VR 360 schedule, relatively small and relatively large ratio requirements occurred. /

II-187

When small ratio requirements occurred, the response rate was (low, high) throughout the ratio; when large ratio requirements occurred, the high rate (was, was not) maintained throughout the ratio. /

high
was not

II-188

Following the high response rate after reinforcement, the decrease in rate during longer ratios may be gradual as at _____ or abrupt as at __● _____. /

a
b

II-189

Careful examination of this record shows that each reinforcing event is followed by a(n) _____ rate, and that the ratio requirements are all (small or large, intermediate). /

high
small or large

II-190

When small ratio requirements are in effect, the high rate leads rapidly to _____. /

90

reinforcement

When large ratio requirements are in effect the rate (increases, decreases) following the _____ post-reinforcement rate. /

decreases
high

It was stated earlier that under VR schedules the contingencies result in a minimal amount of control by _____ generated stimuli. /

behaviorally

In the above case, the contingencies have in essence provided a(n) (one, two, three, four)-valued schedule of reinforcement because most of the ratios were either _____ or _____. /

small
large
(either order)

Therefore, the behavior is under the control of behaviorally generated _____ to a greater extent than generally found under VR schedules of reinforcement. /

stimuli

The development of stable performance could, in such a case, probably be achieved by inserting (small, intermediate, large) ratio requirements into the sequence of ratio values. /

intermediate

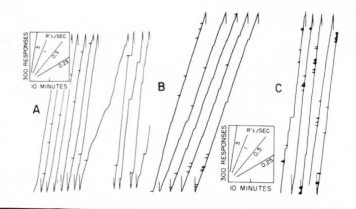

Prior to the record of a pigeon's performance on a VR 110 in *A*, this bird had an extensive past history on variable ratio schedules. /

The overall rate in *A* is approximately _____ responses/sec. Irregularities appear, including alternation between low and high rate and _____●
_____. /

3

pauses

In *B* the overall rate is (higher, lower) than the rate found early in the session in record *A*. Although there is a(n) _____ in rate, the transition from VR 110 to VR 173 has not produced large irregularities in performance. /

lower
decrease

Record C (12 sessions after record *B*) when compared to *B* shows a(n) _____ in rate. /

increase

92

Examination of the records of performance generated by VR schedules shows differences which are a function of the ratio contingencies specified, including (1) the distribution of the ratios (e.g., more small/large/intermediate ratios), (2) whether increases in the mean ratio involved small or large increments, and (3) the length of exposure to a given schedule. /

II-201

The performances generated by instatement of an extinction schedule after VR (as in the case of FR) schedules differ as a function of the past history of reinforcement. /

II-202

The record shows performance generated by an extinction schedule after stable performance on VR 173. /

II-203

The contingencies change from VR 173 to EXT after a. Instatement of the extinction schedule is followed by approximately 1500 responses at the same running rate as generated by the VR 173 schedule. /

II-204

Following a(n) _____ at *b*, the record exhibits overall _____ _____●
_____ (curvature), although the local rate (when responding does occur) is often equal to

the running rate prior to instatement of the extinction schedule. /

pause

negative acceleration

II-205

The primary factor contributing to the decrease in overall rate is _____. /

pausing

II-206

Generally the running rate will be maintained following the transition from a VR schedule to an extinction schedule and the overall rate decrease will be a function of more frequent and longer _____. /

pauses

II-207

The ratio schedules discussed above involve either fixed or variable response requirements. A third type of ratio schedule is the product of a combination of the features of fixed and variable ratio schedules. /

II-208

Since each requirement is fixed, a feature of _____● _____ ratio schedules is utilized; since the size of the ratio increases, a _____ ratio feature is specified. /

fixed
variable

Progressive Ratio
Reinforcement Schedules

II-209

A ratio reinforcement schedule having properties of both FR and VR schedules involves a series of *progressively* increasing FRs. It is, therefore, called a progressive ratio (PR) reinforcement schedule. /

94

If the increment size were five, and the first ratio were FR 5, the progressively increasing ratios would be FR 5, FR 10, FR _____, etc. /

15

The performance on such a _____ ratio schedule will vary with the size of the ratio increment. That is, if each ratio is greater by 40 responses rather than 2 responses, one would expect markedly differing performance. /

progressive

The cumulative records show progressive ratio performance at increments of 2, 5, 10, 20, and 40. Two things are immediately apparent. (1) Over a given session, there are progressively (shorter, longer) pauses. (2) As increment size increases, long pausing tends to occur (earlier, later) and continue for the remainder of the session. /

longer
earlier

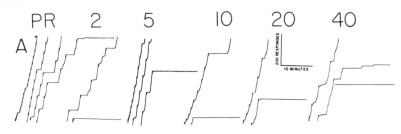

In addition, it appears that the number of reinforcements earned varies with the increment size in a(n) _____ _____ schedule. /

progressive ratio

The figure shows the relation between total rein-forcements per session and ratio increment. /

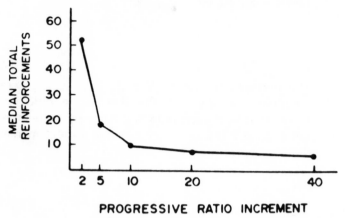

PROGRESSIVE RATIO INCREMENT

The number of reinforcements is inversely related to increment size, with the greatest effect occurring be-tween FR 2 and FR _____. /

5 or 10

We have considered four schedules of reinforcement in which the most important feature in the contin-gencies involved specification of response require-ments. /

These simple schedules in which the primary feature is a number of responses required for reinforcement are (abbreviations) *CRF*, _____, _____, and _____. /

FR
VR
PR

A CRF schedule is one in which each occurrence of

a response of a given class is followed by _____●
_____. /

reinforcement

II-219

A fixed ratio schedule is one in which reinforcement is contingent on the completion of a fixed number of response occurrences, counted from the _____● _____ reinforcement. /

preceding or *last*

II-220

A variable ratio schedule is one in which reinforcement occurs upon completion of a specified number of responses, the number varying from reinforcement to reinforcement. /

II-221

A schedule having properties of both FR and VR schedules, which involves a series of increasing fixed ratios, is called a(n) _____ _____● _____ schedule. /

progressive ratio

II-222

A fifth schedule has been considered which is not a schedule of reinforcement per se, since the contingencies specify that each response occurrence shall go unreinforced. This we call a(n) _____ schedule. /

extinction or *EXT*

II-223

Since each occurrence of the operant requires a minimum amount of time, it may be said that temporal requirements do exist on these schedules. /

II-224

For example, the maximum rate at which a pigeon has been observed to emit the key-peck operant is 10 responses/sec. At this rate under an FR 100 schedule of reinforcement, if sustained responding occurred, the minimum time between reinforcements would be ____ seconds. /

10

II-225

The occurrence of an operant one or more times does require some _____ amount of time. In ratio schedules, temporal requirements do exist, but only implicitly. Control exerted by these schedules is primarily a function of explicitly stated contingencies of response requirements. /

minimum

II-226

We will now consider schedules of reinforcement in which the most salient feature of the contingencies involves explicitly stated _____ (time) requirements. /

temporal

II-227

These simple schedules (like FR, VR, and PR; unlike CRF) are intermittent schedules of reinforcement. /

Objectives

*Variable Ratio
Reinforcement Schedules*

1 What is a variable ratio schedule (definition) and what is the abbreviated notation?
II-148 to II-152, II-166 and II-167
2 Discuss the possible relationship of schedule contingencies and behaviorally generated stimuli under VR schedules. /
II-152 to II-154

3 What is the characteristic rate under VR schedules?
II-155 to II-157

4 What is an important consideration in terms of behavioral effects when selecting the mean ratio size for a VR schedule?
II-161

5 What are the first three values selected in developing a VR schedule, and how are the other values usually selected?
II-158 to II-164

6 Discuss the nature of performance and controlling variables during transition from CRF to VR schedules.
II-168 to II-171, II-176 and II-177

7 Describe characteristic performance generated by VR schedules.
II-173 to II-175, II-178 and II-179, II-180 to II-184

8 The inappropriate selection of VR values may generate irregular performance (and thereby demonstrate the inappropriate value selection). What occurs when there are a number of small and large ratio values but no intermediate values?
II-185 to II-195

9 What are three factors which may affect the performance generated by VR schedules?
II-200

10 What are the effects of instatement of an extinction schedule following characteristic VR performance?
II-203 to II-206

Progressive Ratio
Reinforcement Schedules

11 A progressive ratio schedule programs increasing values of what simple schedules?
II-207 to II-209

12 Over a given session, what is the relation between responding and reinforcement on a progressive ratio schedule?
II-213 to II-215

13 What are the four simple schedules involving explicit response requirements and in what respect do they have implicit temporal requirements?
II-216 to II-221, II-223 to II-225, II-26 to II-33, II-51 to II-55, II-147 to II-151

99

Fixed Interval
Reinforcement Schedules

II-228

A fixed interval (FI) reinforcement schedule is one in which the first response following a specified interval is reinforced. /

II-229

When the contingencies are such that the first response following a fixed interval is reinforced, the contingent relation is referred to as a(n) _____●

_____ _____ reinforce-

ment schedule, abbreviated _____. /

fixed interval

FI

II-230

The contingencies for reinforcement under an FI schedule specify that the *first* response following the interval will be reinforced; implicitly stated is the fact that response occurrences during the interval will go unreinforced. /

II-231

Under the contingencies specified by FI schedules, responses occurring during the specified interval (are, are not) reinforced; the _____ response occurring after the end of the interval is reinforced. /

are not

first

II-232

There are two ways of timing the interval. Successive intervals in fixed interval schedules may be timed from either the delivery of the last reinforcement or from the time when the last reinforcement became available. /

II-233

If each interval is measured from the end of the time

100

at which the last reinforcement became available, the specified "fixed" _____ will be an average about which both shorter and longer intervals will be distributed. /

interval

When each interval is measured from the time of the last reinforcement, the actual time between reinforcements can be (greater, less, greater and less) than the fixed interval value. /

greater

Measurement of the interval from delivery of the last reinforcement will result in no period between reinforcements shorter than the fixed interval. Longer intervals occur because the emission of the _____● _____ (number) response(s) required for reinforcement may not occur immediately following the end of the interval. /

1

When the interval is measured from delivery of the last reinforcement, intervals can occur which are longer than the specified value. Inter-response times which are _____ than the specified value will be (reinforced, unreinforced). /

shorter
unreinforced

The distribution of inter-reinforcement times which might occur when the interval is measured from the time of the last available reinforcement are shown. The specified value of the interval is at _____. /

b

The distribution illustrates interval lengths which could result from timing the intervals from the last reinforcement. The value of the fixed interval is at _____. /

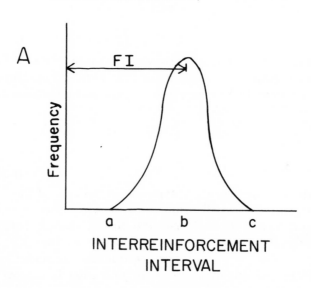

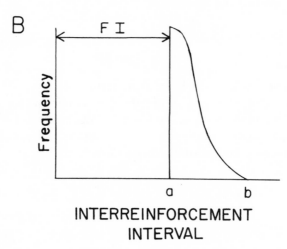

_____

a

It is possible that the differences in performance

could result in a comparison of the two methods for timing the interval. It appears that they are effectively the same (i.e., the performance generated by a given FI schedule is similar whether the interval is measured from the end of the preceding _____, or the occurrence of the preceding _____)./

interval
reinforcement

II-240

In general, schedules in which reinforcement is contingent on response requirements (e.g., FR, VR, and PR) generate a(n) _____ rate, in part because a low rate results in reduced _____ of reinforcement./

high
frequency

II-241

In an FI schedule, a delay of reinforcement is specified by the contingencies. Therefore, schedules such as FI should generate a(n) _____ overall rate./

low

II-242

Fixed-interval schedules differentially reinforce runs of responding preceded by pauses, which results in a(n) _____ _____ rate./

low overall

II-243

In one sense the longer the pauses following reinforcement on a given FI schedule, the higher the probability that the first response will be _____ _____./

reinforced

The above statement is not literally true since the probability does not change gradually. In fact, the probability of reinforcement for a given response instance remains at (0, 1) until the fixed interval has elapsed, when it abruptly changes to (0, 1). /

0

1

The shorthand designation for a given fixed interval schedule includes the abbreviation followed by a number which indicates the length of the specified interval (unless otherwise stated, the unit used is minutes). /

A fixed interval schedule in which the interval specified is 5 minutes would be indicated as _____●

_____ _____. /

FI 5

Indication of the schedule in which the specified interval is 20 seconds would be written as _____

_____ _____. /

FI 20 sec

Shown is a stylized curve of transition from CRF to

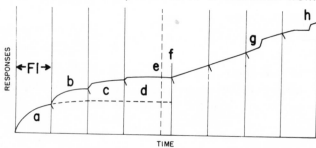

an FI schedule. Reinforcing events are indicated by solid vertical lines from the time axis. /

II-249

The effect of the preceding schedule (i.e., CRF) is seen at *a*, where the curve is _____ accelerated and resembles the performance under a(n) _____ schedule (the extinction curve is illustrated by the dashed line). /

negatively

extinction

II-250

Each portion of the curve at *a* through *d* is negatively accelerated and the number of responses emitted in each interval becomes progressively _____. /

smaller

II-251

The portion of the curve which includes *a* through *d* exhibits overall _____ acceleration. /

negative

II-252

Reinforcement occurs immediately following each of the first three intervals. The fourth interval ends at *e*, but there is a delay of reinforcement until *f* because the required response does not occur until that time. /

II-253

The probability of reinforcement changes from ____● _____ to _____ at the end of each interval. At *e* the probability of reinforcement is _____ and remains so until ____● _____ (where a response occurs and is followed by reinforcement). /

0 (to) *1*

1

f

There is an increase in rate following *f* and a period of relatively constant rate continued to *g*. The occurrence of such a period of increased relatively constant rate during the transition from CRF to FI usually occurs regardless of the length of the _____. /

interval

A period of responding at a relatively _____ rate (e.g., from *f* to *g*) usually occurs in the transition from CRF to FI. The portion of the stylized curve at *g* indicates that the preceding performance (is, is not) stable. /

constant

is not

At *g* a(n) _____ of responding occurs followed by return to a (lower, higher) rate than that found prior to the brief period of high rate. /

burst

lower

At *h* there is a pause followed by a brief period of responding at a(n) _____ rate. /

high

Although not illustrated in the *stylized curve* of transition from CRF to FI, a variable local rate is usually present during the transition. /

The stylized curve shows clearly the component intervals and the overall curve to be _____ accelerated in transition from CRF to FI. /

negatively

II-260

Also illustrated is the period of relatively constant rate occurring in most CRF to FI transitions followed by alternation between bursts, period of moderate rate, and pauses. /

II-261

Shown is the record of transition from CRF to a FI 2 schedule of reinforcement. /

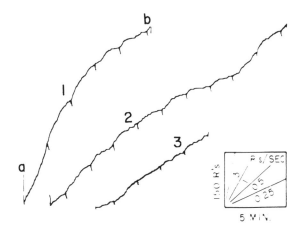

II-262

Initial negative acceleration is evident between _____●
_____ and _____. This portion of the record illustrates the resemblance of CRF to FI transition records to those of CRF followed by a(n) _____ schedule. /

a (and) b
extinction

II-263

The overall rate in this record is intermediate and

107

variable local rate is present throughout the record. /

II-264

The overall rate (decreases, increases) from the first to the third segments, and a change in the response patterning in the intervals is occurring. /

decreases

II-265

The record shows transition from CRF to FI 4, beginning with a pause followed by a burst of responding at *a* and then another _____ of more than 2 minutes. /

pause

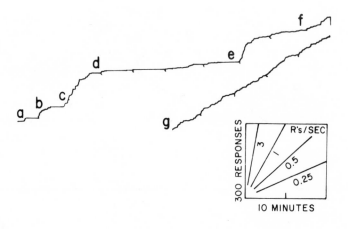

II-266

The first reinforcement under the FI 4 schedule occurs at _____ and is followed by a small _____ accelerated curve. /

b

negatively

II-267

While the successive intervals in the earlier records and stylized curves showed (decreasing, increasing) numbers of responses and (decreasing, increasing) degree of negative acceleration, this record shows more rapid negative acceleration following the first reinforcement than the second and approximately twice as many responses occurring following the second reinforcement as occurring after the first reinforcement. /

decreasing
increasing

II-268

A small burst of responses occurs at *d* followed by long _____ and few response instances between reinforcements until _____, where another small burst occurred, then a pause and a period of responding at _____ rate. /

pauses
e
high

II-269

Segment 2 of this record shows an overall stable (low, intermediate, high) rate; variable _____ _____ is quite apparent (e.g., at *f* and *g*). /

intermediate
local rate

II-270

The second segment of this record is (similar to, different from) the portions of other records produced by later performance during transition to Fl. /

similar to

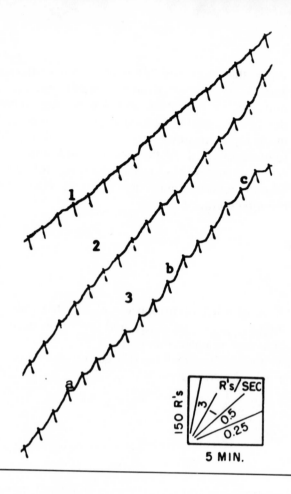

A gradual change of the performance during each interval appears in records during the development of characteristic FI performance, as seen above. /

In segment *1*, brief but irregular pauses and periods of low rate appear; the intervals in segment 2 are characterized by increasing running rate. Periods of decreased rate begin to appear following each _____●
_____. /

reinforcement

The running rate remains high but the periods of

110

decreased rates following reinforcement appear as pauses following reinforcement in segment 3. /

The development of characteristic fixed-interval performance between reinforcements involves (decreased, increased) running rate, a gradually (decreasing, increasing) rate following reinforcement, and finally the development of (shorter, longer) pauses following reinforcement. /

increased
decreasing
longer

II-275

The sequence of a(n) _____ after reinforcement followed by positive acceleration to _____●
_____ rate is characteristic of performance under the contingencies of fixed-interval schedules. When this pattern appears in cumulative records it is referred to as a *scallop* or *scalloping*. /

pause
terminal

II-276

The occurrence of a pattern of responding consisting of a pause after reinforcement and positive acceleration to running rate is called _____ or _____ and results in a moderate overall rate on fixed interval schedules. /

scallop (or) *scalloping*

II-277

Scallops or scalloping is the term given to fixed interval performance exhibiting a pause following reinforcement and positive acceleration to terminal rate. Despite the relatively (low, high) running rate in each interval, the overall rate is _____. /

high
intermediate

II-278

Simple fixed interval schedules with repeated occur-rence of the interval are not commonly found outside the laboratory. One example involved the scheduling of cigarette-smoking behavior with an FI cigarette case. /

II-279

A commercially available cigarette case has a timer which controls a lock on the case. The interval timer may be set at a given value (e.g., 15 minutes). During this interval attempts to open the case are ineffective. At the end of the interval the first case-opening re-sponse is reinforced. That is, the cigarette case may be _____ and a cigarette obtained. /

opened

II-280

Cigarette smoking behavior might be brought under schedule control using this type of cigarette case if the appropriate contingencies for reinforcement were instated. /

II-281

An analysis of the nature of the reinforcer, the stimu-lus conditions controlling the behavior, and the exist-ing schedule must be undertaken prior to instating new contingencies. /

II-282

Stimulus conditions may result in low rate at some times (e.g., "no smoking" signs) and high rate at others (e.g., cocktail parties). Finally, the behavior of reaching for and lighting a cigarette is usually rein-forced on a (CRF, FR) schedule. /

CRF

The instatement of the appropriate schedule in the present instance will permit allowance for the other variables. We know that unwanted alternative behavior may be generated during the _____ from one schedule to another, or by excessive _____ _____ in the schedule value. /

transition

increases

Shown is an example of a "smoker's" IRT distribution. The interval with the highest frequency is the _____ interval (i.e., 10 to __ minutes). /

third

15

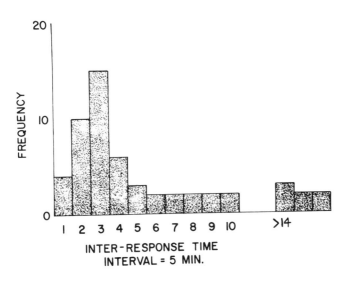

INTER-RESPONSE TIME
INTERVAL = 5 MIN.

Initially to establish use of the cigarette case (and to avoid generating unwanted alternative behaviors) the timer could be set for an interval (shorter, longer) than the most frequent interval in the IRT distribution. Therefore, the timer might be set for (10 minutes, 1 hour). /

shorter

10 minutes

Cigarette-case-opening responses might occur irregularly throughout the interval when the schedule is first instated, although this is made less likely by beginning with a(n) _____ _____•
_____. /

short interval

II-287

As the behavior comes under the control of the contingencies specified by the fixed interval schedule, even in "high-rate" stimulus situations, the occurrence of cigarette-case-opening responses would be most frequent at the (beginning, end) of the interval while _____ would appear at the (beginning, end) of the interval. /

end

pauses

beginning

II-288

When use of the cigarette case and schedule control had been established, the frequency of cigarette-smoking behavior might be decreased by gradually _____ the length of the interval. /

increasing

II-289

In the figure on page 115, the segments shown from the thirteenth session (A), twenty-third session (B), and fifty-sixth session (C) are from a record of pigeon performance generated by an FI 1 schedule of food reinforcement. /

II-290

The records show intervals in which no pauses follow reinforcement and run at high rate through several intervals. /

Compared to records of performance generated by small FI schedules which we saw earlier, these records are (irregular, typical). /

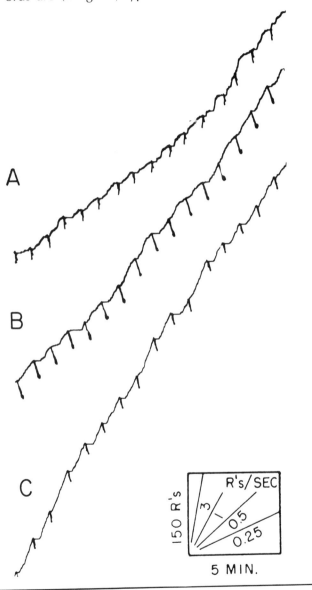

A

B

C

150 R's

R's/SEC

3

1

0.5

0.25

5 MIN.

irregular

These segments occurred as a result of an *accidental contingency* which produced and maintained *superstitious behavior.* /

The sequence of behavior which developed consisted of pecking the panel beside the key before pecking the key itself. Key pecking was reinforced at the end of the interval by food; key pecking served in turn as a conditioned reinforcer for other behavior, which in this case consisted of superstitious panel pecking. /

The maintenance of the _____ behavior involving a(n) _____ contingency is a more probable occurrence under FI than other schedules. /

superstitious
accidental

Characteristic performance under FI schedules which is not present in these segments usually includes a(n) _____ following reinforcement, followed by positive acceleration to the running _____●
_____. /

pause
rate

Fixed ratio schedules tend to result in greater control by behaviorally generated stimuli than variable-ratio schedules. Even greater control by variables other than schedule contingencies can be expected with _____ interval schedules. /

fixed

116

Under an *FR* schedule, superstitious behavior such as pecking the panel beside the key results in reduced frequency of reinforcement since _____ requirements are not completed; under an FI schedule, with the exception of one response at the end of each interval, pecking beside the key is as effective as pecking the key itself. /

response

Organisms under the contingencies specified by FI schedules may develop superstitious behaviors of a high degree of stereotypy which consume a relatively constant period of time following reinforcement. It appears that these "timing" behaviors constitute the portion of the record which we see as a(n) _____● _____ after _____. /

pause
reinforcement

Superstitious behavior occurring due to accidental contingencies is more likely to be maintained under schedules which involve fixed rather than _____● _____ contingencies because of greater control by behaviorally generated stimuli; and under schedules involving _____ rather than response requirements. /

variable
temporal

In addition, since fixed interval schedules involve two factors which together result in greater likelihood of maintenance of _____ behavior, the development of stable performance on fixed interval schedules is more difficult to achieve and records with irregularities are more frequent than under other simple schedules of reinforcement. /

superstitious

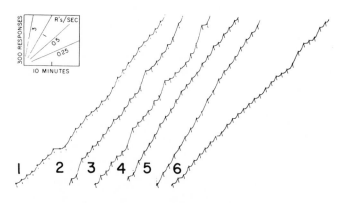

II-301

The record segments shown illustrate sustained performance under an FI 1 schedule. /

II-302

In segments *1* through *5* the overall rate remains fairly constant and relatively consistent; FI _____ _____ is present. /

scallop or *scalloping*

II-303

In the sixth segment there is a(n) _____ in overall rate which is due primarily to longer ____ _____ after reinforcement, prior to the assumption of terminal rate. /

decrease

pauses

II-304

The segments in Frame II-301 illustrate FI performance which is stable after fewer sessions (segment 6 is from the sixteenth session) than found in the preceding record, where after fifty-six sessions performance was unstable due to an accidental contingency which resulted in _____ behavior. /

Irregularities in Fixed Interval
Reinforcement Schedules

II-305

Shown are three single intervals which illustrate characteristic fixed interval performance and common types of rate changes from the pause to running rate. /

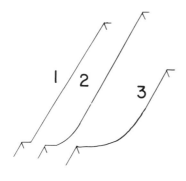

II-306

At *1* the pause following reinforcement is followed by an abrupt change to the _____ rate. /

running

II-307

While at *1* the pause is followed by a(n) _____● _____ change to running rate, in the interval at 2 the running rate is reached through rapid acceleration. /

abrupt

II-308

In the interval at *1* there is abrupt change to terminal rate; at 2 there is _____ acceleration to the running rate. At 3, however, there is (no, gradual) acceleration to the running rate. /

rapid
gradual

Although all three segments illustrate intervals produced by characteristic performance under an FI schedule, the "best" example of FI performance, including a relatively long pause prior to acceleration to the running rate, is seen at _____. /

3

As mentioned earlier, although it is not literally true that probability of reinforcement increases as the interval goes on, the scallop as found in segment 3 indicates greater (schedule, behavioral) control, since reinforcement cannot occur until the end of the interval. Many more unnecessary responses are represented in the example of abrupt change at _____● _____ and rapid acceleration at ____● _____. /

schedule
1
2

Fulfillment of contingency requirements of FI performance would actually not consist of a scallop; it would involve the emission of _____ (number) response(s) following the end of the interval. /

1

As seen in the records thus far, approximations of performance approximating fulfillment of FI schedule requirements (are, are not) frequent. /

are not

Shown are five intervals which illustrate common performance irregularities found under fixed-interval schedules. /

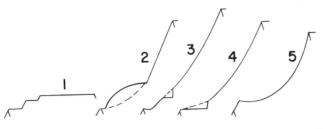

The interval at *1* is an example of what we referred to earlier as a (scallop, knee). It is characterized by a decreasing rate to zero followed by an abrupt change to _____ _____. /

knee

running rate

In 2 there is an abrupt decrease in rate to zero. The pause is followed by a burst of responses at high rate. This sequence and specifically the burst of responding may be referred to as a(n) _____. /

knee

Performance resulting in the type of deviation which appears in segment 3 is usually due to the occurrence of an incompatible behavior (e.g., the behavior occurring upon the presentation of novel stimuli). This sequence does not alter overall rate. /

In the fourth interval following a pause after reinforcement, there is a response burst followed by an abrupt change to a lower rate and then positive acceleration to reinforcement. As in segment 3, it is evident that this sequence does not alter the value of the _____ rate. Evaluation of the record must include consideration of such (local, overall) deviations. /

overall
local

II-318

The fifth interval illustrates *running through,* a phenomenon characterized by responding at the running rate to reinforcement and continuation of this rate through and after reinforcement. /

II-319

Continuation of the running rate through and past reinforcement is referred to as _____ _____. /

running through

II-320

The irregularity illustrated in segment _____ is referred to as a "knee." This deviation may follow the irregularity seen in the fifth interval, which is referred to as _____ _____. /

2
running through

II-321

The irregularities illustrated in segments *1* and *2* are called _____. /

knees

II-322

In the record shown on the opposite page, we witness performance by the gelding, discussed earlier, under an FI 3 schedule of reinforcement. /

II-323

The pauses after reinforcement are in all cases longer

than the 30-second period required to consume the
reinforcer. /

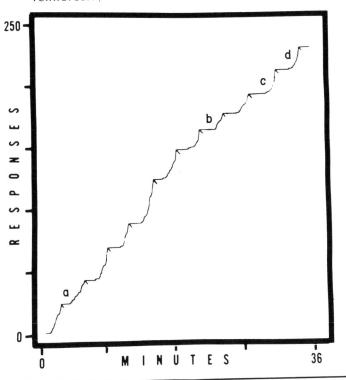

II-324

Some irregularities are present. Variable _____●
_____ rate is apparent in several of
the intervals, especially in the second one at _____●
_____; and at *b* a knee occurs. /

local

a

II-325

Two particularly well-formed scallops occur at _____●
_____ and _____. /

c (and) *d*

II-326

During transition from one value of FI to another, we

123

may expect to find knees, running through, and local rate variability. /

II-327

Although the abovementioned irregularities are expected to appear in the transition from one value to another of FI, it is also expected that the overall performance (will be, will not be) characteristic of FI schedules. /

will be

II-328

During the transition from one value of FI to another, there is a gradual change from control by one schedule value to control by the other. /

II-329

In fact, we find that during the transition the performance is the result of the contingencies of both the original value and the value of the new fixed-interval schedule. /

II-330

After an extended period during which performance is a function of the contingencies of the original and the new FI schedule, stable performance appropriate to the (original, new) schedule will emerge. /

new

II-331

Since performance on FI schedules is, to a great extent, under the control of _____ ___●
_____ _____, rather than schedule control, greater variability in performance as seen in the records is to be expected. /

behaviorally generated stimuli

124

As seen in the records examined thus far, considerable variability exists in the performance generated by FI schedules. This is particularly true under longer fixed-interval contingencies. /

Although in many respects dissimilar, there may be some functional similarities between the contingencies specified by an FI schedule and the procedure called time out, or _____. /

TO

As indicated earlier, stimulus conditions associated with the schedule, the opportunity to respond and the reinforcement contingencies, may be temporarily removed. For example, the subject may be removed from the experimental situation, or the lever may be removed from the test chamber. A period during which the opportunity for reinforcement is removed is called a(n) _____ _____●
_____ and is abbreviated _____. /

time out
TO

Technically a time out is defined as the time during which the organism characteristically does not engage in the behavior being studied. A time out may be achieved in several ways, depending on the organism, the past history, and other variables. /

Since pigeons will not peck a key in the absence of light, it is convenient to arrange a time out simply by turning off the lights in the apparatus. With mammals, a time out can be achieved through the use of a previously developed discriminative stimulus. /

We have also learned that under fixed-interval schedules of reinforcement, the first response after a designated interval of time is followed by the occurrence
of a(n) _____ event. /

reinforcing

Under both the contingencies specied by a fixed
interval schedule and in the condition referred to as
time out (from reinforcement), there is a period
during which reinforcement (does, does not) occur. /

does not

By combining the contingencies specified by an FI
schedule and the condition referred to as time out,
it is possible to effect greater control over an organism's behavior; the resultant behavior more closely
approximates that of "good" (i.e., optimal) performance. /

In the following figures, we will see that the principal
effects of a TO after reinforcement on FI schedules
are (1) reduced frequency of running through, (2) all
intervals begin with pauses, and (3) a decrease in the
overall rate. /

The following figure is composed of segments of performance on an FI 45. The first 20 minutes of each
45-minute interval includes a 20-minute time out.
Therefore, the segments are the product of a schedule which would be labeled TO 20 FI 25. /

The vertical line indicates the point, following which
the schedule, and FI 25, is in effect. Therefore, it is
at this point that the _____ _____
_____ condition is no longer in effect. /

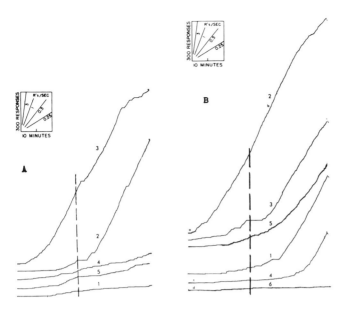

time-out

The segments on the left are from the first session of TO 20 FI 25. With the exception of the third interval, the rates to the left of the vertical line are (high, low); that is, the rates during the portion of the interval which included conditions of _____ _____ from reinforcement. /

low
time out

II-344

High overall rate is apparent early in the interval in segment 3; this interval as well as the others begins with a(n) _____. /

pause

II-345

In the segments at B, we see the second session of TO 20 FI 25. /

With the exception of the second interval (in which the _____ rate is reached before the middle of the interval), the portion of the segments to the left of the vertical line, during which the time-out condition was in effect, exhibit (high, low) rate. /

running
low

With the exception of the last interval (6), each interval exhibits acceleration to _____ rate. /

running

In examining the early portion of each interval, we find that all cases include a(n) _____, the shortest being at ____ and the longest at ____. /

pause
a
d

Since each reinforcement is immediately followed by a pause, there is no evidence of _____ _____ in the records at *B*. /

running through

In comparison with records examined earlier which were the products of performance on FI schedules without time outs after reinforcement, it is also evident that the above records exhibit a(n) (increase, decrease) in overall rate. /

decrease

Thus, the effects of time out after reinforcement on FI schedules are (1) all segments (intervals) begin with a(n) _____, (2) decline in _____ _____rate, and (3) closer approximations to optimal FI performance. /

pause
overall

Added Stimulus Control

Earlier we considered the effects of added stimuli on fixed ratio performance. The stimulus commonly used to achieve greater control of behavior under FR schedules was referred to as an added _____ _____. /

counter

Added stimuli are also useful in achieving control of behavior on fixed interval schedules. When used on FI schedules the stimulus commonly takes the form of, and is referred to as, a(n) _____ clock. /

added

The diagram illustrates the appearance of an added stimulus appearing on the response key used with pigeons on FI schedules (i.e., a(n) _____ _____). /

added clock

On FR schedules the slit of light increased in size as a function of accumulated response occurrences (therefore, its size was dependent on behavior); on FI schedules the slit of light increases as a function of the operation of the timer (therefore, its size is independent of behavior during the interval). /

If the interval has been measured from the end of the preceding interval, the added clock resets with the interval timer at the end of the interval. When the interval is being measured from the last reinforcement, the added clock may remain at maximum size until a reinforcement occurs. Therefore, although its increase in size during the interval is independent of behavior, termination of the maximum size and resetting to the smallest size is _____ on a response occurrence. /

dependent or
 contingent

The slit of light serving as an added clock is the smallest at the (beginning, end) of the interval and largest at the (beginning, end) of the interval. /

beginning
end

Since behavior on a FI schedule is to a great extent under the control of _____ generated stimuli, the effect of the added clock is a decrease of such control and an increase in external control. /

behaviorally

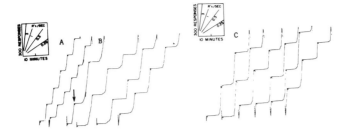

A is the characteristic performance generated by an FI 3 schedule with an added clock. At the arrow (segments at *B*) an FI 6 schedule with clock was instated. *C* is a record of the characteristic performance generated by the FI 6 schedule with an added clock. /

In the FI 3 record at *A*, performance is stable. There is a(n) _____ following each reinforcement which continues through most of the interval; it is followed by a(n) (gradual, abrupt) acceleration to the terminal rate. /

pause

abrupt

At the arrow the contingencies of the FI 6 schedule with added clock are instated. Therefore, the record at *B* is a record of (inversion, transition) from FI with clock to FI 6 with clock. /

transition

In the first interval following instatement of the FI 6 with clock, acceleration to the running rate which prevailed on the _____ schedule occurs and is sustained to the first reinforcement under the new schedule. /

FI 3

The slit of light serving as an added clock now increases in size much more slowly than it did under the FI 3 schedule. The extent to which the clock controls behavior is evident in the lengthened _____●
_____ in the second interval following the arrow and all subsequent intervals. /

pause

The running rate in the transition record (is, is not) the same as that found under the FI 3 schedule with clock. /

is

The only irregularities which occur appear between the pause at the beginning of the _____ and the achievement of running rate. /

interval

The record at C is of characteristic performance under the FI 6 schedule with clock. In the final segment of this record the pauses are (brief, extended) and periods during which responses are emitted are relatively (brief, extended). /

extended
brief

The above records show that an added clock can exert strong control over behavior. In conjunction with the FI schedule, an added clock can generate extremely stable performance with good FI _____●
_____ and relatively few irregularities in the transition from one FI schedule to another. /

II-368

It is evident in the record of transition and the record of characteristic performance under the preceding and new schedule that the performance following the instatement of a new schedule is a function of both the old and new schedules. Control of performance by the new schedule occurs only as a(n) (gradual, abrupt) shift over time. /

gradual

II-369

It is possible to determine the extent to which the behavior is under control of the added stimulus on FI schedules by reversing an added clock. /

II-370

Under the usual conditions of the added stimulus the slit of light (increases, decreases) in size over the interval. Under the reverse conditions the slit of light (increases, decreases) as the interval goes on. /

increases
decreases

II-371

In the figure on the following page, segment *A* is performance generated by an FI 3 schedule with an added clock. At the arrow at the beginning of segment *B*, the clock has been _____. /

reversed

II-372

It is evident that reversal of the clock has occurred because of the inverted scallops and the subsequent change in the appearance of the intervals in the record. /

133

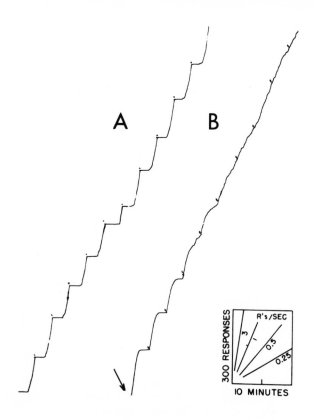

The figure on the opposite page shows segments from the second and third sessions on an FI 10 schedule with an added clock. /

At *A* and *B* the pause is extended and acceleration to running rate is gradual. /

In the segments at *C* and *D*, the pause is (longer, about the same) as found in *A* and *B* but the running rate is (lower, higher) and acceleration to running rate is more (gradual, abrupt). /

about the same
higher
abrupt

134

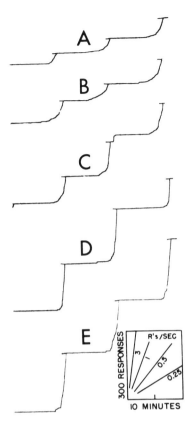

300 RESPONSES

R's/SEC

3

0.5

0.25

10 MINUTES

In the segment at *E*, the pauses are only slightly longer than those found in the earlier segments; however, the acceleration to running rate is becoming extremely (gradual, abrupt), and in the last interval *E* is characteristic performance on the FI 10 schedule with clock. /

abrupt

The above example and earlier discussion of the effects of added stimuli (e.g., added counter on FR, added clock on FI) indicate that they initially function as novel stimuli. Introduction of such stimuli disrupts ongoing behavior and reduces the rate of all behavior. /

The use of added stimuli initially results in reduction in rate since they function as _____ stimuli. The decrease in behavioral disruption generated by such stimuli is referred to as _____● _____. Subsequently, these stimuli may be used to increase control of behavior. /

novel

adaptation

Reinforcement is not contingent on added stimuli, and therefore it is possible that no improvement in behavioral control will occur. The above examples of performance on FI schedules with added clock and the earlier examples of performance on FR schedules with added counters show that the added stimuli usually produce closer approximation to optimal performance. /

The extent to which added stimuli control behavior may be determined by altering the stimulus while maintaining the contingencies for reinforcement constant. A determination of the effect of an added counter (or clock) may be accomplished by _____● _____ the counter (or clock). /

reversing

Records of performance in which the added stimulus has been reversed following the establishment of external behavioral control usually appear to be an (inverted, depleted) version of the records generated prior to the reversal. /

inverted

Objectives

1 What is a fixed interval schedule (definition) and what is the abbreviated notation?
II-228 to II-231, II-245 to II-247

2 What are the two ways of timing the interval and what behavioral differences result from the methods?
II-232 to II-239

3 Describe the overall rate and the component aspects of FI contingencies which generate this rate.
II-240 to II-249

4 What general statement can be made about overall rate in comparing ratio and interval schedules?
II-240

5 Describe the performance during transition from CRF to FI schedules.
II-248 to II-260, II-261 and II-262, II-265 to II-271

6 What is FI scallop and what definable components contribute to the appearance in the cumulative reward?
II-275 to II-278

7 What steps might be taken to decrease the frequency of a high rate behavior using the contingencies of an FI schedule?
II-279 to II-288

8 What is an accidental contingency?
II-292 to II-298, II-301 to II-304

9 What is superstitious behavior?
II-292 to II-298, II-301 to II-304

10 Are accidental contingencies and superstitious behavior more likely to occur under interval schedules than ratio schedules?
II-296 to II-300

11 Describe several irregularities which may occur in single intervals under FI schedules.
II-305 to II-321

12 What is running through?
II-318 and II-319

13 What is a knee?
II-320

14 Describe the transition performance from one to another FI schedule and possible controlling variables.
II-326 to II-330

15 What is a time out and how may it be used to improve FI performance?

II-333 to II-340, II-341 to II-351, also I-78

16 How may an added stimulus be used in conjunction with FI schedules and what is the effect on, and relation to, behavior?
II-352 to II-358

17 What effect does an added clock have on transitions to longer FI schedules?
II-359 to II-368

18 Compare the covariation between responding and contingencies when added stimuli are used in conjunction with FR and FI schedules.
II-355

19 Compare FI performance with and without an added clock.
II-274 to II-277, II-359 to II-370

20 What effect does added clock reversal have on FI performance?
II-371 and II-372

21 What is the initial effect of an added clock on FI performance?
II-377 and II-378

22 What manipulation can be used to determine the extent of stimulus control with an added stimulus?
II-380 and II-381, also I-39 to I-42

Variable Interval
Reinforcement Schedules

II-382

Earlier we discussed fixed ratio and variable ratio schedules of reinforcement. The primary feature and similarity between these schedules lies in the fact that both have, as their primary feature, _____●
_____ requirements. /

response

II-383

The preceding section has dealt with fixed interval schedules in which the primary feature involves ____●
_____ requirements. /

temporal

138

Next we will consider the performance generated by a schedule which is analogous to a variable ratio schedule but has as its primary feature temporal requirements. This schedule is referred to as a variable interval schedule. /

A variable interval (VI) reinforcement schedule is one in which the intervals vary in length from interval to interval in a random or nearly random order. Only after the end of the interval is a response reinforced. /

When the contingencies specify that a response will be reinforced at the end of an interval, the length of which varies from interval to interval, they specify a(n) _____ _____ or ___●
_____ (abbreviation) reinforcement schedule. /

variable interval
VI

Under the contingencies of a variable interval reinforcement schedule, the length of successive intervals varies. Therefore, behavior is subject to greater control by the schedule and less control by behaviorally ___●
_____ _____. /

generated stimuli

Variable interval reinforcement schedules specify that the response shall be reinforced at the end of an interval the length of which varies from interval to interval. /

Behavior generated by ratio schedules is controlled to a greater extent by the schedule than by behaviorally generated stimuli. In general, behavior maintained by all simple variable schedules is controlled to a greater extent by the _____ than by _____ •

_____ _____ _____ •

_____. /

schedule

behaviorally generated stimuli

II-390

While FI performance is to a great extent under the control of behaviorally generated stimuli, we would expect that VI performance is primarily under the control of the _____. /

schedule

II-391

VI schedules tend to generate intermediate rates; and since the conditions change from interval to interval, behavior is primarily under schedule control. Therefore, VI schedules should tend to generate relatively (unstable, stable) performance. /

stable

II-392

Unusual variable ratio performance results if the extreme ratio values are disproportionately represented in the distribution. Unusual variable interval performance may occur if the extreme _____ •

_____ values are disproportionately represented in the distribution. /

interval

II-393

The values in a variable interval schedule are specified by first determining the value of the mean _____ •

_____ and the extreme interval values. /

II-394

Hence, in designing a variable interval schedule, the _____ interval and the _____●
_____ values of the distribution of intervals are first specified. /

mean

extreme

II-395

To determine the interval values either an arithmetic or a geometric progression is usually used. In determining these values we must also consider the *step size.* /

II-396

In addition, in designing a variable interval schedule the step size and the value of the intervals (usually using an arithmetic or geometric progression) must also be specified. If a geometric progression is used, the progression for generating the values (rather than a step size) in the series is determined. /

II-397

Having established the values of the schedule, the order of these values is usually randomized; thus, a schedule has been developed in which variation in length occurs over successive intervals. /

II-398

A variable interval schedule is designated by the abbreviation VI followed by a number indicating the length of the mean interval. If this value is 2 minutes, the schedule would be designated as _____
_____. A variable interval schedule in which the mean interval is 30 seconds would be written as _____ _____
_____. (Recall the standard time unit used and procedure when the time is indicated in other units.) /

VI 2

VI 30 sec

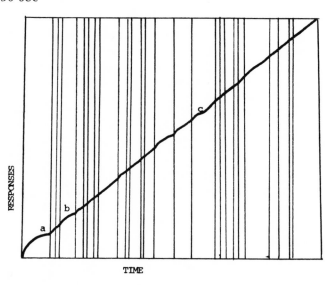

RESPONSES

TIME

The stylized record shown illustrates the transition from CRF to VI. Since the defining feature of a VI schedule involves temporal requirements, reinforcements are indicated as lines extending from the axis labeled _____. /

time

The record shown illustrates that instatement of a VI schedule after CRF (like other intermittent schedules) results in an initial period of (high, low) rate followed by _____ acceleration. /

high

negative

Immediately following the first reinforcement at _____●
_____ there is a(n) _____
in rate. /

a

increase

As was true of the earlier records of transition to other intermittent schedules, the first portion of the record is similar to that found when a(n) _____● _____ schedule is instated. /

extinction

During several of the longer intervals (e.g., at *b*) _____● _____. _____ reappears. /

negative acceleration

Although portions of the stylized record of transition. to VI after CRF exhibit negative acceleration, the overall curve illustrates relatively constant (high, intermediate, low) rate. /

intermediate

The record shows the early development of performance by a pigeon under VI 1 contingencies specified by an arithmetic series of intervals ranging from 0 to 120 seconds in steps of 10 seconds. /

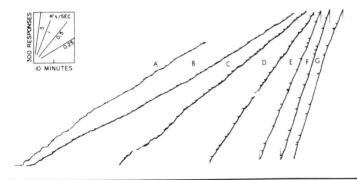

In the first half of the first segment *(A)* there are a

number of successive portions of the record exhibiting oscillation between negative and positive acceleration, while in the later segments there are few such sequences. /

II-407

In segment *B* the overall rate is moderate and stable. Positive acceleration follows initial negative acceleration in the early portion of segment *C*. In the later portion of segment *C* a relatively constant rate of about _____ responses/sec appears. /

0.5

II-408

The rate increases over the session to *E*, after which it remains at about _____ responses/sec, which is constant. /

1.0

II-409

The characteristic performance (e.g., *E*, *F*, and *G*) is primarily under _____ control and there is no evidence of cyclic change correlated with any specific feature of the schedule. /

schedule

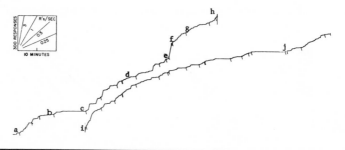

II-410

The performance in the record shown, generated by a VI 2 schedule, is extremely irregular. The values selected were 0, 30, 120, 60, 240, 230, 120, 10, 240, 180, 0, and 210 seconds. /

The transition record of CRF to VI 2 has successive occurrences of negative acceleration. The first example is from _____ to _____, followed by a similar portion (c to d), each with instances of local negative acceleration similar to that resulting from instatement of a(n) _____ schedule. /

a (to) b
extinction

II-412

The probable reason for the irregular performance, especially the extinction-like record, is the inclusion of a large proportion of (short, long) interval values in the schedule. /

long

II-413

The records at A and B are the second and third sessions after CRF on the VI 2 schedule. /

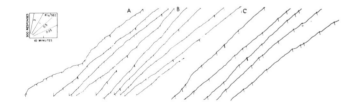

II-414

The second session under the schedule (A) (does, does not) begin with a period of negative acceleration. The third session (B) (does, does not) begin with an initial portion of negative acceleration. /

does
does not

As performance develops under the contingencies of a VI schedule, the period of negative acceleration at the beginning of the session is (eliminated, maintained). /

eliminated

The performance in the fourth session (C) is more characteristic of that maintained by VI schedules, exhibiting intermediate rate. /

Under the contingencies of a VI schedule the behavior generated is closely correlated with the distribution of intervals. /

A schedule including many small and large but few intermediate intervals will generate bursts of responding after each reinforcement since it is frequently followed by another _____. /

reinforcement

In a schedule without intermediate intervals, if a reinforcement does not follow shortly after the previous one, the next reinforcement will not be forthcoming for an extended period. After many sessions, schedule control will be apparent. Following the post-reinforcement burst of responses, the rate will ____●
_____ if a long interval has been programmed. /

decrease

Since the performance generated by VI schedules constructed of dichotomous interval values is irregular, it is of great importance to select the schedule parameters with care. /

Poorly constructed VI schedules result in _____●
_____ performance, which is predict-
able and under schedule control. For example, the
lack of a greater proportion of intermediate values
results in the period of low rate which follows the
period of (high, low) rate after reinforcement. /

unstable
high

For example, if the mean interval and upper extreme
of a series are rapidly increased while the proportion
of small intervals is rapidly decreased, (constant,
irregular) performance will usually result. /

irregular

The effects of large abrupt increases in size of the
ratio (on FR), the size of the mean ratio (on VR), and
the interval (on FI) have already been discussed and
shown to produce (stable, irregular) performance. /

irregular

The record of transition from VI 3 to VI 7 is the first
of the three we will consider which are the product
of performance on a VI 7 having as its longest interval
45 minutes while short intervals have been omitted. /

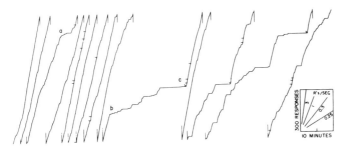

147

The first interval on the VI 7 is relatively (short, long). The effect of this interval is seen at _____, where the record begins to take on the appearance of performance generated by a(n) _____ _____. /

long

a

extinction schedule

Increased reinforcement frequency maintains a constant rate through the next several segments until schedule control is again lost in the middle of a long interval at _____. /

b

A brief period of stabilized performance is again seen following a period of increased _____ of reinforcement after c. /

frequency

The breakdown of schedule control occurs rapidly and the last three segments reveal the irregular performance maintained by this schedule. /

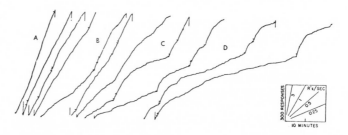

The record shown is the product of another bird's performance on the VI 7 after 240 hours. *A* shows the start of the session; at *B* are segments from the third hour; at *C*, the seventh hour; and at *D*, the end of the session (after 10 hours). /

II-430

There is an overall (increase, decrease) in rate which is accompanied by the appearance of increasingly irregular performance. /

decrease

II-431

In this record following reinforcement there is a(n) _____ in rate. This is followed by a gradual (decrease, increase) in rate. /

increase
decrease

II-432

The irregular performance is attributable to an excessive increase in the value of the mean interval due to the addition of a greater proportion of (shorter, longer) intervals and the deletion of a large proportion of (shorter, longer) intervals. /

longer
shorter

II-433

Several general statements may be made at this point regarding schedule control and irregular performance under simple ratio and interval schedules (i.e., FI, VI, FR, VR). /

II-434

In general, large increases in the size of the mean

(or fixed) unit, and a high proportion of large to small units on variable schedules, can be extremely important factors in generating (stable, irregular) performance. /

irregular

Large increases in the size of the mean unit on VR and VI schedules or fixed unit on FR and FI schedules and the small proportion of small to large units on variable schedules will generally lead to a loss of _____ control and _____ performance. /

schedule
irregular

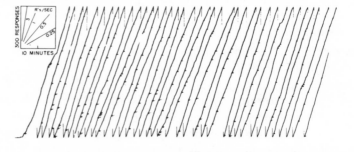

The constant rate shown in the record is characteristic of performance generated by a schedule in which the contingencies specify that reinforcement occurs on a (fixed, variable)-interval schedule. /

variable

The most desirable feature of VI schedules for investigating schedule parameters is seen in the constant intermediate rate sustained for an extended period. /

150

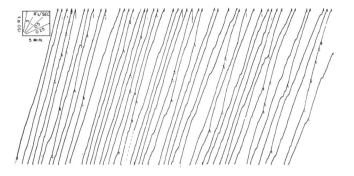

The record of performance on a geometric VI reinforcement schedule includes about 40,000 responses. /

The most noticeable feature of the above record is
the relatively (irregular, stable) performance throughout the session. /

stable

As in some of the earlier records of VI performance,
a rate (increase, decrease) occurs after some reinforcements. Later in the session the frequency of pauses
increases. /

increase

In examining records of VI performance, several
irregularities have been noted, and the figure shows
segments from the records of pigeon performance
exhibiting typical irregularities. /

In the figure on the following page, the segments at *A*
show constant moderate rate generated by the VI
schedule when stable performance prevailed. *B*
through *E* show several types of irregularities. /

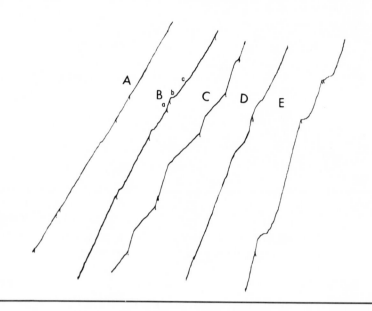

II-443

The segment at *B* illustrates a brief rate (increase, decrease) after reinforcement (at *a*) followed by an abrupt (increase, decrease) in rate (at *b*) and a subsequent change to an intermediate rate (at *c*). /

increase
decrease

II-444

Such a sequence commonly occurs when there is a large proportion of larger and smaller intervals with few intermediate-sized intervals; the effect is similar to that found when variable ratio schedules are used including (one, two, three, four) values. /

two

II-445

In the segment at *C*, there is no pause following the period of (increased, decreased) rate after reinforcement. Rather there is a return to a running rate (at *a*). /

increased

152

In the segment at *D* a common irregularity takes on an appearance much like that found at *C*. However, one difference is apparent; while in *C* there is a(n) (abrupt, gradual) change to an intermediate rate, in the segment at *D* there is a(n) (abrupt, gradual) change to an intermediate rate. /

abrupt
gradual

In the segment at *E* there is an unusual deviation. Following two of the reinforcements, rate abruptly (increases, decreases). /

decreases

In the segments at *B, C,* and *D,* rate increase follows reinforcement. The primary difference in the irregularities appears following the increase in rate. There is an abrupt change to an intermediate rate in the segment at ____, an abrupt change to a low or zero rate in the segment at ____, and a gradual decrease in rate in the segment at ____. /

C
B
D

The most effective way of eliminating irregularities is the instatement of a time out after reinforcement. On removal of the time-out condition, extremely constant and stable performance can be sustained for extended periods. /

In the figure on page 154, the record at *A* illustrates VI 7 performance following the removal of a time out which had been instated to establish stable performance. *B* is a record of irregular VI 7 performance prior to use of the time-out procedure. /

The performance in the record at *A* exhibits greater stability than the record at *B*. Although the irregularities may reappear, it is possible to eliminate irregularities by instating additional IRT contingencies or a

_____. /

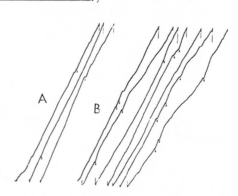

---

time out (or *TO*)

The record at *B* exhibits (more, fewer) deviations than at *A,* and the period between deviations is (greater, less) in the record at *B.* /

more
less

Stable VI performance may be achieved by the temporary instatement of an additional IRT contingency or a TO. However, after extended subsequent exposure to the VI schedule, the previous irregular performance may _____. /

reappear

Progressive Interval Reinforcement Schedules

In an earlier section we discussed *progressive ratio*

154

schedules in which the value of a ratio increases with each successive _____ . /

reinforcement

II-455

A comparable schedule can be programmed with interval schedules in which the value of each successive interval is (increased, decreased). /

increased

II-456

Such a schedule is called a(n) _____ interval (PI) schedule. /

progressive

II-457

The increases can be linear (i.e., each interval is 1 minute longer), or the increases may be of different values (e.g., FI 2, FI 6, FI 10). The figure shows sample cumulative records of progressive interval performance. In this case, another response is available which terminates the progression and returns the schedule to FI 2. Notice the characteristic FI scallops, although the running rates are (lower, higher) than might be expected with a simple FI schedule. /

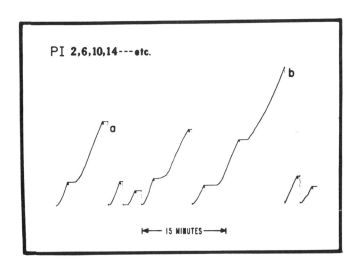

155

higher

II-458

Schedules in which the primary specification is in terms of temporal requirements include (abbreviations) _____, _____, and _____. /

FI
VI
PI

II-459

A schedule in which the first response following a specified and fixed interval of time is reinforced is called a(n) _____ _____ schedule. /

fixed interval

II-460

Variable interval schedules specify temporal requirements which vary in length from interval to interval, and only after the end of the interval is a response reinforced. /

II-461

A schedule which incorporates features of both fixed and variable interval schedules, so that each successive interval increases in value, is called a(n) _____● _____ _____ schedule. /

progressive interval

Objectives

Variable Interval
Reinforcement Schedules

1 What is a variable interval schedule (definition) and what is the abbreviated notation?
II-385 to II-388, II-398
2 What are the probable relations between variable and fixed

schedules with respect to schedule control and control by behaviorally generated stimuli?
II-389 to II-391

3 What is the characteristic rate generated by VI schedules?
II-391, II-404

4 As in the case of variable ratio schedules, irregular performance may be generated as the result of certain combinations of schedule values. What is one particularly important feature having this effect?
II-392, II-418 to II-421, II-442 to II-444

5 What are the steps in developing a VI schedule?
II-393 to II-398

6 Discuss the nature of performance during transition from a CRF to a VI schedule.
II-399 to II-408

7 Describe characteristic VI performance.
II-414 to II-417, II-436 to II-439

8 As in the case of VR schedules, large increases in the mean value of a VI schedule will have effects on performance. What is the effect?
II-422 and II-423, II-429 to II-432

9 Describe several irregularities which may appear in cumulative records of VI performance.
II-442 to II-448

10 Aside from modifying the values of a VI schedule, what is one way in which irregularities may be at least temporarily eliminated?
II-449 to II-453

Progressive Interval
Reinforcement Schedules

11 A progressive interval schedule programs increasing values of what simple schedules?
II-454 to II-456

12 What are the simple reinforcement schedules in which the primary specification is in terms of temporal requirements?
II-458 to II-461

Inter-Response-Time
Reinforcement Schedules

In discussing simple schedules, it was stated that ratio schedules differentially reinforce high response rates, while interval schedules differentially reinforce low rates. This terminology may be misleading, since the schedules are defined in terms of times and numbers of responses, not response rates. /

II-463

Certain schedules have been designed to more closely approximate differential reinforcement of low and high rates, and have generally been designated differential reinforcement of low rate schedules or differential reinforcement of high rate schedules. The former is abbreviated DRL, the latter _____. /

DRH

II-464

In a DRL schedule, reinforcement occurs following the first response after a fixed interval from the preceding reinforcement, with premature responses restarting the time interval again until the specified interval has elapsed without a response. /

II-465

Such a schedule does, indeed, generate low rates. However, it would be more appropriately defined in terms of the schedule contingencies: namely, differential reinforcement of a minimal inter-response time. /

II-466

A similar problem arises in defining DRH schedules, where reinforcement is contingent on responses occurring in less than certain specified inter-response times. /

II-467

Once again, it is true that such contingencies do generate the kind of behavior the name suggests; however, for purposes of consistency, the schedule should be defined by its _____, not by features of performance generated. /

contingencies

II-468

To minimize these problems, DRL and DRH schedules can be considered members of a broader set of contingencies defined as *differential reinforcement of inter-response times,* which can simply be designated *IRT* schedules. /

II-469

Using this nomenclature, a schedule requiring a minimum period between successive response for reinforcement to occur would be designated by IRT, plus a numerical value corresponding to the interval. The fact that a minimum interval is specified is indicated by a "greater-than" sign ($>$) between IRT and the numerical value. Thus, a DRL 5-minute schedule would be written IRT _____, using the suggested nomenclature. /

> 5

II-470

If a schedule were designated as IRT > 30 sec, this would mean that responses spaced 30 seconds or more apart would be reinforced. This would be the same as a DRL _____ schedule. /

30-sec

II-471

A schedule in which responses must be spaced at least 2 minutes apart to be reinforced would be written _____ in the suggested nomenclature. /

IRT > 2

II-472

In some case, contingencies may be arranged such that responses must occur *within* a specified period since the last reinforced response for reinforcement to occur. Such schedules have been called DRH schedules but can be designated in the same notation scheme as other IRT schedules. A DRH 10-sec schedule would be designated IRT < 10 sec. The "less-than" sign indicates that responses must be spaced less than 10 seconds apart for reinforcement to occur. /

II-473

If the contingencies were such that the maximum period which could elapse between reinforcement and the next response (if another reinforcement is to be obtained) is 3 seconds, the schedule would be specified as _____. /

IRT < *3 sec*

II-474

A complication with such maximum inter-response-time contingencies is that satiation may occur if reinforcement was available every 3 seconds. Usually, several such contingencies must be satisfied, or a specified number of responses must be emitted within the inter-reinforcement interval. /

II-475

A third type of inter-response-time schedule involves both upper and lower limits on the inter-response intervals that will be reinforced. For example, a schedule specifying that responses must be spaced at least 10 seconds apart, but not more than 20 seconds apart, would be designated an IRT > 10, < 20 schedule. /

II-476

It should be noted that such schedules are comparable to what has generally been called DRL schedules with a limited hold. Thus, a DRL 1 minute with a 10-second limited hold is identical with an IRT > 60, < 70-sec schedule. /

II-477

A schedule specifying that responses must be spaced not less than 90 seconds and not more than 2 minutes

apart would be designated a(n) _____
_____ (expressed in seconds) in inter-
response-time scheduling. /

IRT > 90, < 120
 schedule

II-478

As indicated above, IRT schedules were originally
studied because they tended to generate high or low
rates, depending on the contingencies and parameter
values. The cumulative records here show typical
performance on an IRT > 15-sec schedule, which
might also be called a(n) _____ _____●
_____ _____. /

DRL 15-sec schedule

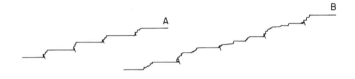

II-479

Notice that the responses are more-or-less regularly
spaced, with occasional bursts of 3 to 4 responses. In
record A these bursts seem to occur at somewhat
regular intervals, while in record B the bursts are
more irregular. Nonetheless, the overall rates are
equal. /

II-480

Thus, overall rates do not tell us all that we might
want to know about behavior maintained by such an
IRT schedule. To gain greater insight into controlling
variables in IRT schedules, it is generally necessary to
use IRT distributions, as discussed in Section I. /

II-481

If _____ distributions were plotted for
responses occurring in records A and B, they would
look somewhat as shown here. /

161

IRT

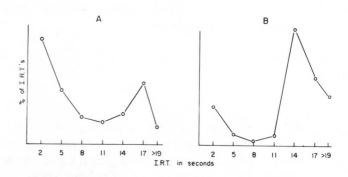

I.R.T. in seconds

II-482

The distribution for *A* is bimodal, with the primary peak at _____ seconds, and a secondary peak at _____ seconds. /

2

17

II-483

The IRT _____ for *B* is also bimodal, with the primary peak coming at _____ seconds. /

distribution

14

II-484

The differences in the two records, while not grossly apparent from the cumulative records and certainly not apparent in overall rates, *did* reveal themselves in the shapes of the _____ distributions. /

IRT

II-485

If we now examine the IRT distributions, and are told that record *B* was from the first session and record *A* was from the 30th session, the records become more meaningful. It would appear that early in condition-

162

ing, animals tend to emit responses varying considerably in inter-response times, while late in conditioning, the variability in inter-response time is (reduced,
increased). /

reduced

Further, late in conditioning there is a marked tendency for responses to be spaced either 15 seconds
apart or _____ seconds apart. /

2

One might wonder why there is such a large proportion of short IRTs even after considerable experience
on the IRT > 15-sec schedule. Since short IRTs are
never reinforced, one would assume that they would
eventually cease occurring. The following figure shows
the first session on an IRT > 18-sec schedule. /

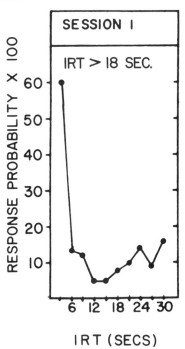

There is a relatively large proportion of short IRTs. One explanation for this continuation of short IRTs is that there is very little consequence of short bursts immediately following reinforcement. That is, a burst at that time only postpones the next reinforcement for a length of time equal to the relatively brief duration of the _____. /

burst

One way of making certain responding at other inter-response times *does* have a consequence is to arrange the schedule such that only responses falling within a specified range of IRTs less the scheduled value (will, will not) be reinforced, and responses spaced more than a specified IRT postpone reinforcement as well. /

will not

In the foregoing case, the contingency might be changed to IRT > 18, < 21. The figure shows the performance after 50 sessions. The very short IRTs have (decreased, increased) while the proportion of IRTs from 18 to 21 seconds has (decreased, increased). /

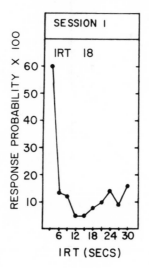
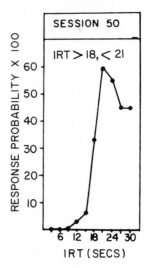

II-491

It is also noteworthy that while relatively more responses are spaced 27 to 30 seconds apart than
before, the peak is (below, within, above) the reinforced IRT range. /

within

II-492

These data suggest that a major controlling variable
for spacing of responses in IRT schedules is the range
of IRTs that will be reinforced. /

II-493

Thus, the high proportion of bursts in the earlier
record appears to be due to the fact that only
one end of the reinforced range was specified. Short
IRTs had (little consequence, markedly postponed
reinforcement). /

little consequence

Temporally Defined
Reinforcement Schedules

II-494

Another group of simple intermittent schedules is pro-
cedurally defined by strictly temporal contingencies
but can generate either ratio-like or interval-like performance, depending on schedule parameters. These
have been called *temporally defined schedules*. /

II-495

In the simplest case, a fixed-interval schedule is programmed with an FI 5 IRT < 5-sec contingency. In
such a schedule, no responses are reinforced during
a 5-minute period of the fixed interval, and the _____●
_____ response occurring during the 15-
second IRT period is reinforced. /

first

If one thinks of the total period of the FI plus the limited hold as a "cycle," it becomes apparent that the longer the maximum of the added IRT contingency, the greater proportion of each cycle is available for a reinforced response. Indeed, one could express this quantitatively by dividing the limited hold period by the total cycle length, or $FI +$ _____ . /

IRT

As this proportion [i.e., $IRT/(IRT + FI)$] approaches $+1.00$, the schedule would, for practical purposes, be a simple fixed interval schedule, the value of which is equal to FI. /

Consider an FI 1 minute schedule, with an IRT contingency of 59 seconds. The ratio would be $59/59 + 1$, or $+0.98$. One should not expect to find any appreciable difference between this schedule and a simple _____ schedule. /

FI 1

However, as the length of the IRT contingency is shortened, relative to the value of the FI, many possible reinforcements will be missed if responding occurs at a low rate as the time of reinforcement approaches. Thus, as the ratio $IRT/(IRT + FI)$ becomes progressively smaller, response rate _____ . /

increases

Thus, if the FI 1 in the foregoing example had a limited hold of 0.1 minute, the ratio would be $0.1/1.0 + 0.1$, or $+0.09$. Unless response rates were very high, with very short pauses, many reinforcements

166

would be missed. Such contingencies should generate performance like a simple _____
schedule. /

FR

II-501

Another way of expressing the foregoing is that as
the ratio IRT/(IRT + FI) approaches +1.00, performance should resemble that in a simple _____
schedule, whereas as the ratio approaches zero, the
performance should resemble that found in simple
_____ schedules. /

FI
FR

II-502

Consider the following set of fixed interval and
limited hold values, and their corresponding ratios.

FI length	IRT length	IRT/(FI + IRT)
19.5	10.5	0.35
1.5	28.5	0.93
0.9	29.1	0.97
0.6	29.4	0.97
0.4	29.6	0.98

At FI 19.5 IRT < 10.5, reinforcement is available
35 percent of the time. Similarly, at FI 0.4 IRT < 29.6,
reinforcement is forthcoming 98 percent of the time.
From the previous discussion, response rate should
be highest at the (top, bottom) of this chart. /

top

II-503

Performance should be most like simple fixed interval
schedule behavior nearest the (top, bottom) of the
chart. /

bottom

167

The figure shows the response rate as a function of the ratio size. Notice that over ratios from zero to 0.05, the response rate _____ sharply. /

drops or *decreases*

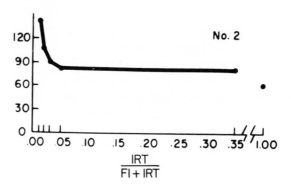

Thus, with relatively short _____ and relatively long _____, we expect rate to be very high. /

IRT
FI

The following cumulative records are details from larger records of sample performance at ratios of 1.00 and 0.05. Notice that at 1.00 performance is more __● _____-like, whereas at 0.05, performance is clearly more _____-like. /

interval
ratio

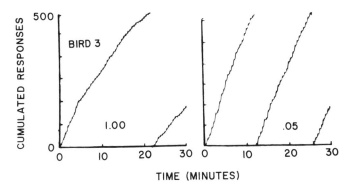

CUMULATED RESPONSES

BIRD 3

1.00

.05

TIME (MINUTES)

Time-correlated schedules such as the foregoing have been called "random ratio" schedules. They obviously are not ratio schedules in the usual sense, because reinforcement is not correlated with the _____ _____ of responses. /

number

With a modification of the conditions from reinforcement, "random ratio" schedules become "random-interval" schedules. /

If the cycle length, or _____ + _____● _____, is held constant, but we arrange contingencies so that reinforcement is not forthcoming during every IRT period, the schedule becomes a random _____ schedule. /

FI + IRT
interval

The probability (P) that the first response during a given IRT period will be reinforced is comparable to the probability of reinforcement on a VI schedule. Thus, the larger the probability (P) that first response will be reinforced, the more it is like a short VI. Conversely, the smaller P is, the more it is like a(n) _____● _____VI. /

long

169

In random interval schedules, response rate varies with both *P* (probability that the first response will be reinforced) and the total cycle length (IRT + FI). The higher *P* is, relative to the cycle length, the more the behavior should resemble fixed interval performance. /

The relation of *P* to cycle length can be expressed as (IRT + FI)/*P*. As reinforcement probability is decreased and cycle length is held constant, the ratio (IRT + FI)/*P* increases. /

As the ratio (IRT + FI)/*P* increases, response rate should decrease, since the likelihood of reinforcement has decreased. /

The figure shows the relation between (IRT + FI)/*P* for pigeons trained on a random interval schedule with cycle length held constant at 5 seconds, at varying reinforcement probabilities or _____ (abbreviation). /

P

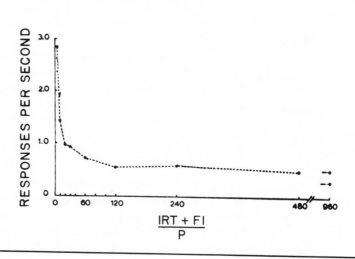

Notice there is an inverse relation between the ratio (IRT + FI)/*P* and response rate. In other words, at a given cycle length (or _____ + _____), the higher the

probability of reinforcement, the _____
the response rate. /

FI (+) IRT
higher

Objectives

Inter-Response Time
Reinforcement Schedules

1 What are the two inter-response time schedules discussed
and what are their effects on behavior?
II-462 and II-463

2 Describe the contingencies of a DRL schedule.
II-464 and II-465

3 Describe the contingencies of a DRH schedule.
II-466 and II-467

4 Why is it considered more useful to refer to DRL and DRH
schedules as IRT schedules?
II-465 to II-468

5 What are the three possible forms of IRT schedules in terms
of specification of minimum and maximum intervals, and
what are the abbreviations describing these schedules?
II-469 to II-477

6 What information about IRT-schedule performance can be
obtained using IRT distributions that cannot be ascertained
using simple rate measures?
II-478 to II-486

7 What contingency could be established to eliminate bursts
of responses?
II-489 to II-493

Temporally Defined Reinforcement Schedules

8 What types of performance (ratio- and/or interval-like) are
most likely to occur under the contingencies of temporally
defined schedules?
II-494, II-501 to II-503, II-511 to II-513

9 What temporally defined schedule contingencies are most
likely to generate FR-like performance?
II-499 and II-500, II-501 to II-503, II-511 to II-513

10 Why have variations of the temporally defined schedules presented been referred to as "random ratio" and "random interval" schedules?
II-507 to II-509

11 What alteration in contingencies would produce a variable temporally defined schedule and what would determine the extent of ratio- or interval-like performance?
II-510

Sidman (Free Operant) Avoidance

II-516

Earlier schedules were discussed in which one response occurring after an interval of specified duration produced reinforcement. The interval length was either constant (fixed interval) or varied around some mean value (variable interval). In both cases the emission of one response following the end of the interval resulted in reinforcement. One schedule involving temporal contingencies which requires the emission of one response *prior* to the end of a specified interval is Sidman or free operant avoidance. /

II-517

Since no external stimuli are programmed, Sidman or _____ _____ avoidance is a case of unsignaled avoidance. /

free operant

II-518

In the free-operant avoidance situation, no external stimuli are programmed except a stimulus known to be an effective negative reinforcer. The negative reinforcer is programmed for presentation at the end of a specified interval specified from the last response (e.g., 10 sec). As the name of the procedure implies, the consequence of a response emitted prior to the end of the interval results in _____ of the stimulus (e.g., shock or loud noise). /

avoidance

II-519

Since the operandum is freely available and the specified avoidance interval is repetitive, the situation in which an organism makes repeated responses to avoid a stimulus is referred to as _____ _____ _____. /

II-520

In the prototypic situation, the interval between shocks when no response occurs (e.g., Shock–Shock interval = 10 sec) and the interval between the occurrence of a response and the next programmed shock (e.g., Response–Shock interval = 10 sec) are equal. /

II-521

The contingencies of the prototypic free-operant avoidance situation specify that a shock will be delivered at regular intervals (e.g., _____- Shock interval = 10 sec or S-S = 10 sec) and that a response occurrence will result in postponement of the shock for a specified interval (e.g., _____ _____-Shock interval = 10 sec or R-S = 10 sec). /

II-522

Additionally, the contingencies of the basic procedure specify that the Shock–Shock (___-___) interval and the Response–Shock (___-___) interval are of (equal, unequal) duration. /

II-523

If the programmed contingencies of the Shock–Shock interval are SS = 10 seconds, the basic free-operant avoidance procedure for each response will postpone shock for an equal interval; that is, the Response–Shock interval will be specified as RS = _____● _____ seconds. /

II-524

To simplify the notation when the two intervals in effect are equal, we simply write ____-____ = ____-____ = 10 seconds. /

S-S (=) R-S

II-525

The figure represents the time course of shocks and responses in the free-operant avoidance situation. /

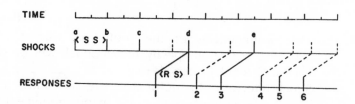

II-526

Programmed shocks occur which have not been preceded by responses; that is, the S-S interval is in effect at *a*, *b*, and ___. Dashed lines indicate potential shocks avoided by responding. /

c

II-527

An R-S cycle and postponement of the programmed shock result from the occurrence of a response at _____. /

1

II-528

Since no response occurs during the R-S interval which began at *1*, an S-S interval begins with the shock at _____. /

d

Each time an interval begins with a shock, we refer to the _____ interval, while each occurrence of a response begins a(n) _____ interval. /

Shock–Shock
Response–Shock

Therefore, the S-S interval which begins at *d* is terminated by the response at 2 and begins a(n) _____● _____ interval. /

R-S

Successive responses at intervals shorter than the specified S-S or R-S intervals postpone shock (i.e., result in shock avoidance). If successive responses occur at intervals greater than the S-S or R-S intervals, a shock is programmed to occur. /

As stated, each shock or response terminates the preceding cycle and instates a new cycle. Therefore, the S-S cycle which began at *d* is terminated by the response at 2, which also begins a new R-S interval. This interval begins with the response at _____. /

3

The response at 3 instates an R-S interval which is terminated by the shock at *e*, which instates a(n) ____● _____interval terminated by another response at 4. /

R-S

Examining the diagram we see that each shock is

preceded by an interval equal to the S-S or R-S interval (see *a-b-c, 1-d, 3-e*). /

II-535

Each shock or response which is followed by a response (i.e., during an S-S or R-S interval) is preceded by a period shorter than an S-S or R-S interval (see *d-2-3, 4-5-6*). /

II-536

Therefore, in the basic procedure (where S-S = R-S), each shock is preceded by a period (shorter than, equal to) the S-S = R-S interval, while each response is preceded by a period following a shock or response which is (shorter than, greater than) the S-S = R-S interval. /

equal to
shorter than

II-537

While organisms can acquire the behavior specified by the contingencies of the basic procedure (S-S = R-S), acquisition is facilitated if the S-S interval is relatively short compared to the R-S interval. /

II-538

Therefore, acquisition of free-operant avoidance behavior would occur if S-S = R-S = 15 sec, but would be more rapid if S-S = (5, 20) and R-S = (5, 20). /

5
20

II-539

In the cumulative records of free-operant avoidance acquisition by a rat, each downward displacement of the pen indicates shock. The contingency generating the acquisition performance at *A* was S-S = R-S = 15 sec, while the contingency at *B* was S-S = 5 sec, R-S = 20 sec. /

176

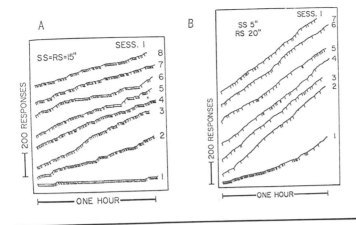

Comparison of the cumulative records at *A* and *B* illustrates that free-operant avoidance acquisition is more rapid when (S-S > R-S, S-S = R-S, S-S < R-S). /

S-S < R-S

The relative length of the S-S to R-S interval can affect acquisition of free-operant avoidance. If the S-S interval is shorter than the R-S interval, acquisition is (facilitated, impaired); conversely, if the S-S interval is longer than the R-S interval, acquisition is (facilitated, impaired). /

facilitated
impaired

In both of these cases the effect of the response becomes a more discriminable event. Therefore, when the S-S is decreased sufficiently relative to the R-S (e.g., S-S = 1 sec, R-S = 10 sec), the situation approaches the contingencies of an escape procedure. However, when the S-S is increased relative to the R-S (e.g., S-S = 10 sec, R-S = 1 sec), the situation approaches the contingencies of a punishment procedure. /

Acquisition is facilitated when the S-S interval is relatively shorter than the R-S interval because the effect of a response is more discriminable. That is, closely spaced shocks (e.g., S-S = 1 sec) no longer occur following a response, when the R-S is long (e.g., R-S = 10 sec). This situation approximates a(n) (escape, punishment) procedure. /

escape

Acquisition is impaired when the S-S interval is relatively longer than the R-S interval, again because the effect of the response is more discriminable. That is, widely separated shocks (e.g., S-S = 10 sec) are presented until a response occurs (if R-S = 1 sec) and the situation then approximates a(n) (escape, punishment) procedure. It appears that the animal is responding differentially to shock density. /

punishment

The relationship between rate and interval length can be demonstrated with the basic free-operant avoidance procedure (i.e., where S-S = R-S). The figure shows the effect of S-S = R-S interval length on response rate. /

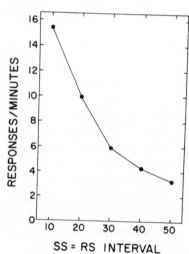

In the figure it is evident that under the contingencies of the basic free-operant avoidance procedure, as the S-S = R-S interval increases, the response rate ____●
_____. /

decreases

The change in response rate as a function of S-S = R-S interval length requires that the organism have contact with the contingencies. In the free-operant avoidance situation, contact with the contingencies requires that the organism receive _____. /

shocks

If the organism responds at a high rate and does not receive shocks, programmed increases in the S-S = R-S interval will probably not affect behavior, while decreases in the S-S = R-S interval will result in a response-rate _____. /

increase

Where maintained free-operant avoidance behavior is established (with S-S = R-S), decreases in the S-S interval alone will have little effect on behavior since the occurrence of shocks will generally be at the end of a(n) _____ interval and temporally remote from the response. /

R-S

During maintained performance the S-S cycle is usually terminated by a response and consecutive shocks do not occur. Therefore, little behavioral change will occur if the S-S interval is _____●
_____. /

decreased

While changes in the S-S interval will have little effect on maintained responding, increases in the R-S interval will have an effect similar to that which occurs when the S-S = R-S interval is increased. That is, there will be a response-rate _____. /

decrease

II-552
The figure illustrates the change in response rate as a function of increases in the R-S interval (from S-S = R-S = 10 sec to S-S = 10 sec, R-S > 10 sec). /

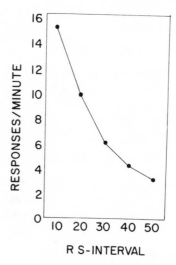

R S-INTERVAL

II-553
The effect of increasing the R-S interval appears as a gradual change in response rate. The rate decrease depends on the organism receiving occasional shocks, thereby having contact with the increased R-S interval. /

II-554
The fact that similar rate decreases occur when S-S = R-S interval increases are programmed and when

180

R-S interval increases are programmed, indicates that established performance is maintained by the _____●_____ length (when S-S < R-S). /

II-555

The rapidity with which a behavioral change will follow a programmed change in interval length depends on the contact with the contingency (i.e., elapsing of the R-S interval). Therefore, if an organism responds at a very high rate, the behavioral change occurs less rapidly than if the response rate is lower. This is illustrated in the figure. /

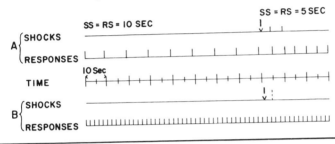

II-556

The shock and response lines at *A* with S-S = R-S = 10 sec indicate no shocks occurring but responses spaced at just less than the the specified contingency. If at the arrow the interval is reduced to S-S = R-S = 5 sec, contact with the contingencies is made and response rate (decreases, remains unchanged, increases). /

II-557

The shock and response lines at *B* indicate no shocks but responses occurring at short IRTs relative to the specified contingency. If at 1 the interval is reduced to S-S = R-S = 5 sec, no contact is made with the contingencies and response rate (decreases, remains unchanged, increases). /

II-558

The difference in response rates and number of shocks received appears to vary as a function of the species used. While rats respond at relatively low rates and take frequent (e.g., 1/3) shocks, monkeys generally respond at high rates and are shocked only infrequently (e.g., 1/500). /

II-559

In the free-operant avoidance situation, it should be expected that behavioral changes as a function of contingency changes will occur more rapidly when the experimental organism is a(n) _____ rather than a(n) _____. /

rat

monkey

II-560

Since monkeys respond at high rates consistently, one situation in which a more rapid change in behavior would occur in this species than in rats would be if the contingency were changed from S-S = R-S = 10 sec to (S-S = 10 sec, R-S = 20 sec; S-S = 10 sec, R-S = 2 sec). /

S-S = 10 sec,
R-S = 2 sec

II-561

The cumulative records shown were generated by a free-operant avoidance contingency which specified S-S = R-S = 10 sec. Monkey performance is illustrated by the segments at _____ and rat performance under the same contingency is illustrated by the segments at _____. /

A

B

II-562

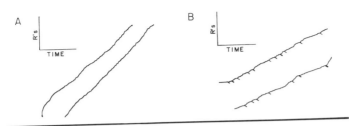

In neither case is typical performance of the two species illustrated above efficient. The performance of the monkey is characterized by few shocks and the emission of (fewer, many more) responses than the contingencies require, while that of the rat is characterized by many shocks and therefore (fewer, many more) responses than required by the contingency. /

many more responses
fewer responses

Aside from consistent species differences, the performance generated by the basic free-operant avoidance procedure is generally consistent in terms of intraorganism behavior but variable between organisms of the same species. /

When fixed ratio and fixed interval schedules were compared, the ratio schedules resulted in performance closer to the optimum for the schedule while performance under interval schedules was to a greater degree under the control of behaviorally generated stimuli. /

In the case of free-operant avoidance performance, the contingencies specify only some minimal response rate required to avoid all shocks. The temporal requirements specify a maximum but not a minimum IRT contingency. /

In this respect the performance generated by free-

operant avoidance schedules is similar to that of ____●
_____ _____ schedules
and is primarily under the control of _____
_____ _____ . /

fixed interval
behaviorally generated
  stimuli

II-567

As in the case of fixed interval performance, relatively efficient performance can be established under free-operant avoidance schedules when added stimuli are programmed by the experimenter. /

Added Stimulus Control

II-568

There are a number of variations on the prototypic Sidman or free-operant avoidance procedure (where S-S = R-S and no added stimuli are programmed). Variations discussed earlier included the cases where the contingencies specified S-S > R-S and S-S < R-S. /

II-569

The presentation of tones or lights as added stimuli which delineate portions of the S-S or R-S intervals in the free-operant avoidance procedure change the situation from one of unsignaled to _____ avoidance. /

signaled

II-570

In one experiment with rats, a tone was presented during the last quarter of the S-S = R-S interval. A comparison of the performance prior to instatement of the added stimulus and stable performance following instatement of the added stimulus is shown in the figure. /

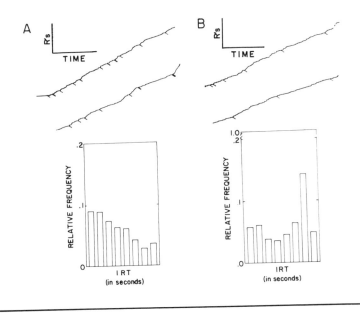

Cumulative record segments and the IRT distribution show performance to be relatively inefficient (i.e., more responses are emitted than required, shocks occur due to failure to appropriately space responses) and that shocks occur more frequently prior to added stimulus instatement (A) than following instatement of the added stimulus (B). /

II-572

More efficient performance resulted when the added stimulus was present during the last quarter of the interval, as indicated by the increased frequency of (short, long) IRTs in the distribution at B. /

long

II-573

Since fewer shocks occurred, despite fewer response occurrences when the added stimulus was present (B), the performance involves more regular spacing of responses and therefore a closer approximation to optimal performance. That is, the added stimulus generated (less, more) efficient performance. /

more

II-574

The change in efficiency of rat free-operant avoidance performance from *A* to *B* is characterized by _____ shocks, _____ responses, and _____ regular spacing of responses. /

fewer

fewer

more

II-575

A free-operant avoidance experiment with monkeys used the sequential presentation of a series of lights to delineate portions of the S-S = R-S interval and temporal distance from shock. /

II-576

Segments of cumulative records and IRT distributions generated by the free-operant avoidance schedule with and without the added stimulus are shown. /

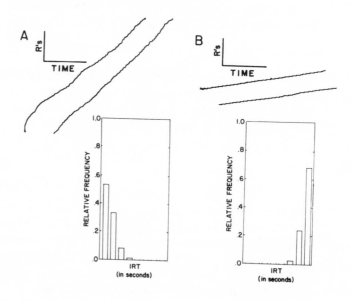

186

II-577

The response rate illustrated in the cumulative record segments is higher in ________________ than in ________________. /

A
B

II-578

The mode of the IRT distribution at *A* is at (short, long) inter-response times, while the mode of the IRT distribution at *B* is at (short, long) inter-response times. /

short
long

II-579

It is evident from comparison of the cumulative records and IRT distributions that the added stimulus was not present at ________________ and was present at ________________. /

A
B

II-580

The more efficient performance of a monkey when an added stimulus is present appears as no change in shock frequency, ________________ responses, and ________________ regular spacing of responses. /

fewer
more

II-581

The species differences which exist in performance under the contingencies of a free-operant avoidance schedule are decreased but still present when added stimuli are programmed. /

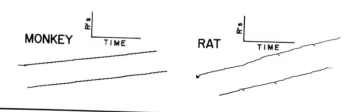

The use of added stimuli in the free-operant avoidance situation results in (less, more) efficient performance by both species. However, differences in performance are (still, no longer) present. /

more

still

II-583

The programming of added stimuli in conjunction with reinforcement contingencies generates more efficient performance. This was illustrated with FR and FI schedules and in the preceding discussion of free-operant avoidance. /

Analysis of Maintained Free-Operant Avoidance Behavior

II-584

An analysis of free-operant avoidance performance is unlike that for other avoidance paradigms in several respects. /

II-585

Recall that the basic procedure is unlike other avoidance procedures in that (1) it provides continuous repetition of the contingencies rather than discrete trials, (2) it does not provide explicitly programmed stimuli other than shock, and (3) it involves a brief inescapable shock rather than a shock which can be terminated by an escape response. /

II-586

There are procedural differences between other avoidance paradigms and free-operant avoidance with regard to (1) continuous repetition of the _____● _____ rather than discrete trials, (2) absence of explicitly programmed _____, and (3) duration and termination of _____. /

contingencies
stimuli
shock

These procedural differences and the resulting behavior create a unique situation. Performance is maintained in a situation which (1) involves no response-contingent stimulus change except omission of shock, (2) involves reinforcement delay for the duration of the R-S interval, and (3) operationally reinforcement involves the *nonpresentation* of a stimulus. /

Since the procedure provides for postponement rather than termination of shock, a response occurrence (does, does not) produce an immediate stimulus change. /

does not

In addition to the lack of stimulus change, there is, for the duration of the R-S interval, a reinforcement _____. /

delay

Finally, the procedure specifies that reinforcement consists of the (presentation, nonpresentation) of a stimulus. /

nonpresentation

Explanation and analysis of the free-operant avoidance procedure must consider the following features of maintained performance: (a) no immediate response contingent _____ change, (b) reinforcement delay for the _____ interval duration, and (c) reinforcement through ____•_____ of a stimulus. /

stimulus

R-S

nonpresentation

Interpretations of the factors maintaining free-operant avoidance performance have been based on (1) the development of conditioned aversive responses, (2) shock-density-reduction discriminations, and (3) temporal discriminations. /

The explanation through *conditioned aversive responses* suggests that all behaviors other than the specified operant are punished. That is, when the organism engages in any behavior other than the specified operant, shocks are (avoided, presented). /

presented

All behaviors other than the specified operant are punished, and therefore these nonavoidance behaviors themselves take on aversive properties through pairing with shock. /

According to the conditioned-aversive-response explanation of free-operant avoidance, the specified operant occurs at a relatively high rate since all other behaviors develop aversive properties through ____•_____ with shock. /

pairing

II-596

Therefore, the specified operant is emitted relatively frequently since the consequence of all other behaviors is (reinforcement, punishment). /

punishment

II-597

The explanation of free-operant avoidance based on the conditioned aversive properties of behaviors other than the specified operant is referred to as the ●

_____ _____ _____

_____ explanation. /

conditioned-aversive-
  response

II-598

A similar interpretation hypothesizes the development of conditioned-aversive-temporal stimuli (CATS). /

II-599

The conditioned-aversive-temporal-stimuli explanation preposes that the passage of time, measured from discriminable events, generates stimuli. /

II-600

According to this explanation, events in the environment, including shocks and responses, produce stimuli which provide for discriminations based on the passage of _____ . /

time

II-601

Since these proposed temporal stimuli are differentially correlated with shocks, they differ in aversiveness. /

It is suggested that the development of conditioned-aversive-temporal stimuli, in relation to the S-S and R-S intervals, results in (differential, equal) aversiveness for all periods. /

differential

Since periods closer to shock (and further from a response) are thought to be more aversive than periods immediately following a response, it is argued that greater reduction in aversiveness and therefore greater reinforcement occurs if there is a delay between responses. /

The conditioned-aversive-temporal-stimuli explanation of maintained free-operant avoidance performance asserts that the temporal stimuli are differentially _____ and that greater reinforcement results if there is a(n) _____ between responses. /

aversive
delay

The explanation which suggests that differentially aversive temporal stimuli are conditioned and that delays between responses result in greater reinforcement is referred to as the _____ ____●
_____ _____ ____●
_____ (CATS) explanation. /

conditioned-aversive-
temporal-stimuli

The *shock-density-reduction* explanation of free-operant avoidance performance suggests that changes in shock frequency are discriminable and that response-produced reduction in shock frequency maintains performance. /

II-607

Unlike the conditioned-aversive-response and conditioned-aversive-temporal-stimuli explanations, the shock-density-reduction explanation does not hypothesize the existence of aversive stimuli in the form of response-produced stimuli or temporal factors. /

II-608

The shock-density-reduction explanation proposes that reduction in shock frequency resulting from avoidance responses is sufficient to maintain avoidance behavior and that there is no need to invoke stimuli in the form of _____ _____●
_____ or _____ factors. /

response-produced
temporal

II-609

The shock-density-reduction account of free-operant avoidance behavior suggests that the sufficient condition to maintain avoidance behavior is reduction of
_____ _____. /

shock frequency

II-610

Explanation of avoidance behavior produced by decreased shock frequency is referred to as the _____●
_____ _____ _____●
_____ explanation. /

shock-density-reduction

II-611

The free-operant avoidance situation and other avoidance paradigms differ with regard to (1) repetition of _____ rather than discrete trials, (2) absence of explicitly programmed _____, and (3) duration and termination of _____. /

193

contingencies
stimuli
shock

II-612

These procedural differences require an explanation of free-operant avoidance behavior that accounts for performance involving (1) no immediate response contingent _____ changes, (2) reinforcement delay for the _____ interval duration, and (3) reinforcement through _____ of a stimulus. /

stimulus
R-S
nonpresentation

II-613

Three suggested explanations of the factors maintaining free-operant avoidance performance have been discussed, based on conditioned-aversive _____● _____, conditioned-aversive-_____● _____ _____, and shock-_____ _____. /

responses
temporal stimuli
density reduction

II-614

The explanations based on conditioned-aversive responses and conditioned-aversive-temporal stimuli (do, does not) invoke additional stimulus sources, while the explanation based on shock-density reduction (does, does not) invoke such stimuli. /

do
does not

Objectives

1 Describe the contingencies of a Sidman or free-operant avoidance schedule.
II-516 to II-524, II-526 to II-538

2 What variations in the temporal parameters of a free-operant avoidance schedule facilitate and which variations impair acquisition?
II-537 to II-538, II-539 to II-541, II-541 to II-542

3 Describe the effects on rate of manipulating the temporal parameters of a free-operant avoidance schedule from essentially an escape contingency to a punishment contingency.
II-537 to II-544, II-546 to II-550

4 While major changes in the formal contingencies may have a rapid behavioral effect, there are certain changes which may have little effect on avoidance behavior. What are these changes and under what conditions would the changes have little effect on behavior?
II-546 to II-550

5 As under other schedules, performance "appropriate" to the temporal parameters of an avoidance schedule requires occasional behavior-contingency contact (and hence shocks). Under what conditions will behavior be unlikely to change as a function of parameter changes?
II-547 to II-551, II-555

6 Species similarities and differences may exist with respect to some features of performance under avoidance schedule contingencies. Discuss them.
II-558 to II-563

7 Describe the effects of introducing an added stimulus on a free-operant avoidance baseline.
II-570 to II-581

8 How does Sidman or free-operant avoidance differ from other avoidance procedures?
II-518, II-585 to II-590

9 Discuss the conditioned-aversive-response hypothesis as it applies to free-operant avoidance.
II-592 to II-597

10 Discuss the CATS hypothesis.
II-598 to II-605

11 Discuss the shock-density-reduction hypothesis.
II-606 to II-610

12 What factors must be accounted for by formulations intended to explain avoidance behavior?
II-591, II-612

195

13 Which formulations describing factors controlling avoidance behavior invoke additional stimulus sources, and which formulations do not?

II-614, II-592 to II-597, II-598 to II-605, II-606 to II-610

References

II-38 Stylized curve of operant level, CRF schedule, and EXT schedule.

Drawn by authors.

II-48 Cumulative record of extinction of operant vomiting.

Ullman, L. P., and Krasmer, L. (eds.), *Case Studies in Behavior Modification*. New York, Holt, Rinehart and Winston, 1965.

II-61 Stylized curve of CRF to FR transition, pigeon.

Ferster, C. B., and Skinner, B. F., *Schedules for Reinforcement*. New York, Appleton-Century-Crofts, 1957, Fig. 12, p. 42.

II-67 Cumulative records of performance of CRF to FR transition, pigeon.

Ferster and Skinner. Fig. 14, p. 44.

II-75 Performance at several FR values, horse.

Myers, R. D., and Mesker, D. C., "Operant Responding in a Horse under Several Schedules of Reinforcement." *Journal of the Experimental Analysis of Behavior*, 3, No. 2 (April, 1960), 161–164.

II-79 Cumulative record of performance on FR 60 and EXT, pigeon.

Ferster and Skinner, Fig. 22, p. 50; Fig. 31, p. 58.

II-86 Cumulative record of characteristic performance on FR 200 and FR 120, pigeon.

Ferster and Skinner, Fig. 24, p. 52.

II-98 Cumulative-record segment showing irregularities, including variable post-reinforcement pause and knees, pigeon.

Ferster and Skinner, Fig. 25, p. 53.

II-101 Cumulative-record segments showing irregularities of variable post-reinforcement.

Ferster and Skinner, Fig. 27, p. 55; Fig. 30, p. 57.

II-109 Cumulative record showing irregularities due to insufficient reinforcement, pigeon.

Ferster and Skinner, Fig. 41, p. 65.

197

and development of VI performance, pigeon.
Ferster and Skinner, Fig. 386, p. 327.

II-410 Cumulative record of irregular performance on VI sched-
Ferster and Skinner, Fig. 389, p. 329.
ule, pigeon.

II-413 Cumulative record of early performance on VI 2 schedule, pigeon.
Ferster and Skinner, Fig. 390, p. 329.

II-424 Cumulative records of irregular performance during and
after transition from VI 3 to VI 7 schedule, pigeon.
Ferster and Skinner, Fig. 406, p. 340.

II-429 Cumulative record of irregular performance generated
by VI schedule with poor value distribution, pigeon.
Ferster and Skinner, Fig. 408, p. 341.

II-436 Cumulative record of sustained VI performance during
a 9-hour session.
Ferster and Skinner, Fig. 404, p. 339.

II-438 Cumulative record of characteristic performance on geometric VI schedule, pigeon.

II-441 Cumulative-record segments illustrating irregularities and
local rate changes on VI schedule, pigeon.
Ferster and Skinner, Fig. 401, p. 337.

II-450 Cumulative record of VI performance before and after
use of TO to eliminate irregularities.
Ferster and Skinner, Fig. 428, p. 353.

II-457 Cumulative-record segments of PI schedule performance.
Findley, J. D., "Preference and Switching under Concurrent Scheduling." *Journal of the Experimental Analysis of Behavior, 1,* No. 2 (April, 1958), 123.

II-478 Stylized curves showing IRT schedule performance.

II-481 IRT frequency distributions of IRT schedule performance.

II-487 IRT frequency distribution for first session on IRT > 18-sec
schedule.
Kelleher, R. T., Fry, W., and Cook, L., "Inter-response
Time Distribution as a Function of Differential Reinforcement of Temporally Spaced Responses." *Journal
of the Experimental Analysis of Behavior, 2,* No. 2
(April, 1959), 91–106.

II-490 IRT frequency distribution for performance on IRT > 18,
< 21-sec schedule.
Kelleher, R. T., Fry, W., and Cook, L., "Inter-response
Time Distribution as a Function of Differential Reinforcement of Temporally Spaced Responses." *Journal
of the Experimental Analysis of Behavior, 2,* No. 2

(April, 1959), 91–106.

II-504 Response rate as a function of ratio size on temporally defined schedule.

Farmer, John, "Properties of Behavior under Random Interval Reinforcement Schedules." *Journal of the Experimental Analysis of Behavior*, 6, No. 4 (Oct., 1963), 607–616.

II-506 Cumulative-record segments of performance on IRT schedule.

Hearst, E., "The Behavioral Effects of Some Temporally Defined Schedules of Reinforcement." *Journal of Experimental Analysis of Behavior*, 1, No. 1 (Jan., 1958), 45–55.

II-514 Relationship between $(IRT + FI)/P$ on random-interval schedule.

Hearst, E., "The Behavioral Effects of Some Temporally Defined Schedules of Reinforcement." *Journal of the Experimental Analysis of Behavior*, 1, No. 1 (Jan., 1958), 45–55; Fig. 3, p. 50.

II-525 Relationship between responses and shocks on Sidman (free-operant) avoidance schedule.

II-539 Cumulative-record segments of free-operant avoidance acquisition with equal and unequal temporal parameters, rats.

Sidman, M., "Avoidance Behavior," in *Operant Behavior: Areas of Research and Application*, W. K. Honig, ed. New York, Appleton-Century-Crofts, 1966.

II-545 Rate of avoidance responding as a function of (S-S = R-S) temporal parameter duration, rats.

Verhave, Thom, "Avoidance Responding as a Function of Simultaneous and Equal Changes in Two Temporal Parameters." *Journal of the Experimental Analysis of Behavior*, 2, No. 3 (July, 1959), 185–190; Fig. 2, p. 186.

II-552 Rate of avoidance responding as function of (R-S) temporal parameter duration.

II-555 Dependence of avoidance-response-rate change (following parameter change) on ongoing rate.

II-561 Cumulative-record segments comparing avoidance performance differences as functions of species, monkeys, rats.

Grabowski, J., Ph.D. thesis, 1970; Fullmer, W., unpublished data.

II-570 Avoidance performance without added stimulus, rat.

Fullmer, W., unpublished data.

II-576 Avoidance performance without added stimulus, monkey.
Grabowski, J. Ph.D. thesis data, 1970.

II-582 Cumulative-record segments comparing avoidance performance differences with added stimuli as functions of species differences, monkeys, rats.
Grabowski, J., Ph.D. thesis data, 1970; Fullmer, W., unpublished data.

SEQUENTIAL AND CONCURRENT REINFORCEMENT SCHEDULES

SEQUENTIAL SCHEDULES

Chaining and Chained Reinforcement Schedules

III-1

Operant responses frequently occur in regular sequences in which each response produces proprioceptive stimuli for the next response. Since these response-produced stimuli are not accessible, it is difficult to specify the controlling stimuli in behavior sequences. /

III-2

A useful method of studying stimulus functions in sequences of operant behavior involves using exteroceptive response-produced stimuli. Such stimuli, unlike proprioceptive or interoceptive stimuli, are accessible for observation and manipulation by the experimenter. /

III-3

By arranging reinforcement contingencies such that responding in the presence of one exteroceptive stimulus produces a second exteroceptive stimulus, and responding in the presence of the second stimulus leads to unconditioned reinforcement, a procedure for studying stimulus functions in a sequence of operant behaviors or operant *chain* is provided. /

III-4

A reinforcement schedule with two or more components in succession, with a discriminative stimulus for each component and unconditioned reinforcement following completion of the sequence, is called a(n) _____ reinforcement schedule. /

chained

III-5

In chained reinforcement schedules, the last component is followed by unconditioned _____. /

reinforcement

III-6

When responses occur in the presence of a discriminative stimulus and produce the discriminative stimulus for another operant, the process is called operant _____. /

chaining

III-7

The response class in each of the operants of a chain may be the same, in which case the sequence is called a *homogeneous* chain; or they may be different, in which case the sequence of operants is called a *heterogeneous* chain. /

III-8

Whether the response classes of the successive operants in a chain are the same [a(n) _____ chain] or different [a(n) _____ chain], the behaviors appropriate to the chain must be shaped. /

homogeneous
heterogeneous

III-9

A chained schedule is established in which a monkey pulls a chain on a VI 4 schedule in a darkened chamber, which leads to the presentation of a light setting the occasion for a bar pressing reinforced on a VI 4 schedule reinforced with food. This procedure is an example of a (homogeneous, heterogeneous) chain. /

heterogeneous

III-10

The discriminative stimulus for the first VI 4 schedule which indicated that the _____ _____●
_____ response class leads to reinforcement was "dark." The conditioned reinforcer for the emission of members of this class was the onset of "_____," which also serves as a discriminative stimulus for the emission of the _____●
_____ - _____ response class. /

chain-pull
"light"
bar-press

III-11

It is important to note that the conditioned reinforcer for one operant in a chain may serve as a discriminative stimulus for the next operant in the chain. In the above example, onset of light, which serves as the _____ _____ for the chain-pull response class, also serves as a(n) _____●
_____ _____ for instances of the bar-press response class. /

conditioned reinforcer
discriminative stimulus

III-12

Emission of the bar-press response has as its reinforcing event the presentation of the (conditioned, unconditioned) reinforcer, _____. /

unconditioned
food
204

The completion of the bar-press response class under a (VI, FI) schedule is reinforced by the presentation of food. /

VI

While the first response is the chain pull and the second is the bar press, this two-operant chain is established in the reverse order. That is, _____● _____ _____ing is conditioned in the light on a CRF and then a VI schedule; the rat is then placed in the dark; emission of the chain-pull response produces the conditions for the second operant, early in the procedure under a CRF schedule, later under a(n) _____ schedule. /

bar press(ing)
VI

When establishing a sequence of behaviors under a chained schedule, conditioning is begun with the (first, last) component. At the end of each component in a chained schedule of reinforcement (except the last), there is a discrete stimulus change which serves as a(n) _____ _____● _____ for the preceding operant and a(n) _____ _____ for the operant which is to follow. /

last
conditioned reinforcer
discriminative stimulus

Reinforcement Frequency and Performance in Chained Schedules

In chain schedules the response or temporal requirements of each component may be manipulated independently. For example, a chained schedule with 2 VI schedule components can be established in which the first component involves a chain-pull response reinforced on a VI 4 while the second member involves a bar-press response reinforced on a VI schedule the value of which is manipulated by the experimenter. /

III-17

In VI schedules the number of reinforcements per unit time for each component varies as a function of the value of the schedule. In the foregoing example, the value of the second component is being manipulated. /

III-18

In interval schedules, increasing the length of the interval decreases the possible *frequency of reinforcement,* while decreasing the interval length (increases/ decreases) the possible frequency of reinforcement. /

increases

III-19

Thus, if the second member of a two-member chain is changed from VI 50 to VI 10, the frequency of reinforcement has (increased, decreased). /

increased

III-20

If the second member of a two-component chain is changed from VI 30 seconds to VI 8 minutes, the possible frequency of reinforcement has (increased, decreased). /

decreased

III-21

The reinforcing properties of stimuli associated with subsequent members of chained schedules depend, in part, on the *frequency of reinforcement* associated with those stimuli. /

In the foregoing example, if the mean value of the VI schedule in the first operant was held constant and the mean value of the VI schedule in the second operant was varied, under the longer mean VI schedules in the second operant the rate during the first operant will be lower. /

The figure shows the total response output per reinforcement as a function of the mean VI used with the second operant. The points connected by the solid line are from the first series of value changes; those connected by the dashed line are from repetition of the sequence on the same subject. /

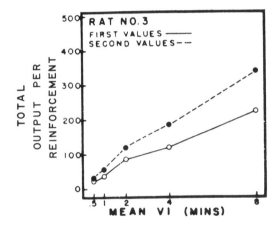

It is evident that as the length of the mean VI increased, the total response output per reinforcement in the second operant (decreased, increased). /

increased

This study shows that the properties of the (first, last) operant in a sequence have a systematic effect upon the (prior, later) operants in a sequence; and

207

that chaining procedures and intermittent reinforcement contingencies result in greater behavioral outputs. /

last
prior

III-26

In a study using pigeons, the discriminative stimulus for the first operant was a white light and the discriminative stimulus for the second operant was a green light. The mean length of the VI schedule was held constant for the second operant and varied for the first operant. /

III-27

The figure shows the response rate for one bird during the white and green conditions as a function of the mean VI schedule used in the white conditions [i.e., the (first, second) component]. /

first

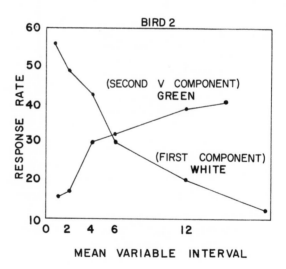

III-28

As the mean-variable-interval length in the first operant increases, the rate in white decreases, while the rate in green (decreases, increases). That is, as the length of the mean VI interval of the first component increases, the rate in the first component decreases, and the rate in the second component (decreases, increases). /

increases

increases

The figure shows at A the FI performance in the second operant when the schedule in the first operant is a VI 4 and at B the FI performance in the second operant when the schedule in the first operant is a VI 20. /

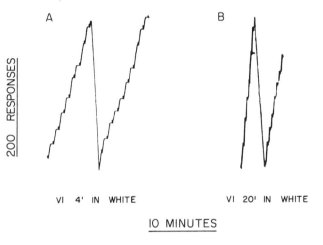

VI 4' IN WHITE   VI 20' IN WHITE

10 MINUTES

From the above records it is apparent that increasing the length of the mean VI in the first operant (decreases, increases) the rate in the second operant. /

increases

The examples cited above and other studies in this area indicate that the effects of the conditions in an early component in a sequence on later components is less than the effect of the conditions in later components. That is, stimulus conditions and contingencies for reinforcement of the components closest to the _____ reinforcer have a greater effect on the preceding components than stimulus conditions and contingencies for reinforcement of an early component on later components in the chain. /

unconditioned

Reinforcement Probability and Performance in Chained Schedules

III-32

In ratio schedules, lowering the ratio value increases the *probability of reinforcement,* while increasing the size of a ratio (increases, decreases) the probability of reinforcement. /

decreases

III-33

If the second member of a two member chain is changed from FR 50 to FR10, the probability of reinforcement has (increased, decreased). /

increased

III-34

The reinforcing properties of stimuli associated with subsequent components for preceding components of chained schedules also depend on the probability of reinforcement. /

III-35

For example, compare the probability of reinforcement during the second components of the following two chained schedules: (A) Chain FI 1 FR 50 and (B) Chain FI 1 FR 200. The probability would be higher during the second component of chain _____●
_____ (A or B). /

A

210

It would be expected, therefore, that the discriminative stimulus for the second component of chain B would serve as a (less, more) effective conditioned reinforcer than the discriminative stimulus for the second component of chain A. /

less

The following examples show the effects of changing the size of the fixed ratio in the first, second, and third components. /

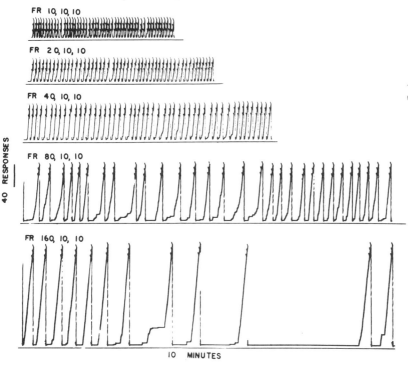

The figure shows records of performance under a three component chained fixed ratio schedule. The ratio values of the second and third components were constant while the value of the first component had, over successive sessions, the values *10, 20,* _____, _____, _____. The pen of the recorder resets following each completion of the chain. /

III-39

The records show that as the ratio on the first component increased, the length of the pause preceding resumption of responding in the _____ component increased (i.e., following the presentation of the unconditioned reinforcer). /

first

III-40

The performance in the first component in the chain (is, is not) disrupted and the performances in the second and third components in the chain (are, are not) disrupted by the increase in the size of the ratio in the first component. /

is

are not

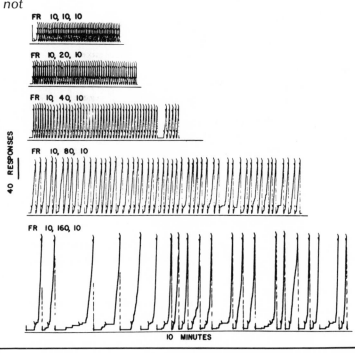

III-41

These records show the performance under a three component chained schedule in which the value of the _____ ratio increased. /

III-42

Increase in ratio size in the second component resulted in some pausing following the first component, but in general the performance of the second component was maintained. At the largest ratio value of the second component, considerable disruption of performance of the (first, third) component occurred. /

III-43

The increase in the value of the ratio of the second component had some effect on performance in that component and severe effects on the performance in the _____ component. Performance in the third component (was, was not) disrupted. /

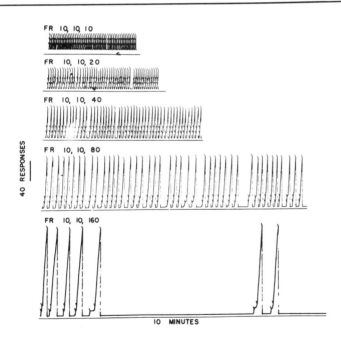

FR 10, 10, 10

FR 10, 10, 20

FR 10, 10, 40

FR 10, 10, 80

FR 10, 10, 160

40 RESPONSES

10 MINUTES

first
was not

213

The effect of increasing the size of the fixed ratio in the third component of this three component chain is increased _____ preceding resumption of responding in the first component. /

pausing

Although there is an increase in the length of the pause in the first component and some disruption in the first and second components, the increase in the size of the fixed ratio of the third and last component has almost no effect on performance in this component. /

The preceding examples show that the effect of an early operant in a sequence upon later components is (less, greater) than the reverse case. The component in a chain most severely affected by the increase in the size of the fixed ratio in the component is the (first, second, third). /

less
first

It is important to note that the length of the pause prior to resumption of responding is in part a function of the component's relation to the occurrence of unconditioned reinforcement. Disruptive effects of changes in the schedule of reinforcement will in general appear in the _____ component in a chain. /

first

In summary, the two main classes of factors determining the reinforcing properties of stimuli in chained schedules are (1) _____ and _____ of reinforcement and (2) _____•

_____ to unconditioned reinforcement. /

probability (and)
  frequency
proximity

III-49

The _____ the probability and frequency of reinforcement, the greater the reinforcing properties of stimuli present during those contingencies. /

greater

III-50

And, the nearer a given component and its correlated stimulus are to the unconditioned reinforcer, the __● _____ the conditioned reinforcing properties developed by the stimulus. /

greater

Tandem Schedules

III-51

A schedule with two or more components in succession, with no discriminative stimulus correlated with the schedule, and with reinforcement following completion of the terminal component is called a *Tandem* reinforcement schedule. /

III-52

A schedule in which reinforcement follows the fifth response emitted after an interval of 10 minutes had elapsed would be called a tandem schedule and would be abbreviated Tand _____. /

FI 10 FR 5

III-53

The foregoing tandem schedule (Tand FI 10 FR 5) has

a corresponding chained schedule, Chain FI 10 FR 5, which differs from the tandem schedule in that the chained schedule has _____ _____●
_____ associated with the FI 10 and the FR 5 components. /

discriminative stimuli

III-54

Any differences between the Tand FI 10 FR 5 and Chain FI 10 FR 5 cannot be attributable to the contingencies for reinforcement, since they are identical. Therefore, differences in performance between the two schedules must reflect the role of the _____●
_____ _____. /

discriminative stimuli

III-55

Because of this feature, tandem schedules are often used to facilitate interpretation of stimulus function in _____ reinforcement schedules: that is, whether they serve as discriminative and/or conditioned reinforcing stimuli and the strength of these properties. /

chained

III-56

For example, pigeons were trained first on Tand FI 3 FI 2 and then on Chain FI 3 FI 2. The stimulus presented during the FI 2 component of the chained schedule was present during both components of the tandem schedule. /

III-57

The figure illustrates the transition from tandem to chained schedules (i.e., from A to A'). Diagonal pip marks indicate component completion; dots indicate schedule completion and unconditioned reinforcement. In the tandem schedule, responding tended to be positively accelerated between food reinforcements, and performance resembled that occurring in

216

a simple schedule rather than a two component schedule. In the chained schedule, positively accelerated responding occurred in (the first, the second, each) component, establishing characteristic performance at d. /

each

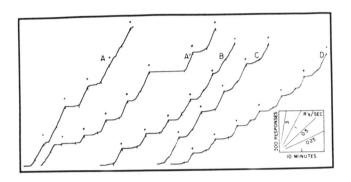

Thus, it appears that the light presented during the second component FI 2 was a(n) _____ _____ for responding in the presence of the first component stimulus. /

conditioned reinforcer

In the foregoing fashion, _____ functions in chained schedules can be interpreted, using tandem schedules. /

stimulus

Since tandem schedules are exclusively under the control of the _____ contingencies, any differences between components of a tandem schedule must be due to the type and values of the schedules in effect. /

schedule or
 reinforcement

Of the many possible combinations of simple schedules, those involving combinations of two values of
fixed ratio contingencies, or two values of variable-
ratio contingencies, become trivial. Consider the
scheduling of FR 10 and FR 50 in tandem. The resulting schedule effectively becomes an FR 60. In the
two records shown here, the curve labeled A is a(n)
_____ FR 10 FR 50, while the curve
labeled B is a(n) _____ FR 10 FR 50. /

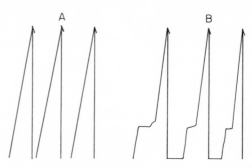

tandem
chained

Combinations of ratio and interval contingencies may
not, however, be trivial. The behavior generated by
such contingencies often reveals marked and important differences. /

Unlike combinations of two FR schedules, the order
of the interval and ratio components in Tand FI FR
schedules can be an important variable. In addition,
the values of the interval length and ratio size can
significantly influence overall performance as well
as behavior in each component of the tandem
schedule. /

If, for example, we examine Tand FI FR performance

where both components have relatively small values (e.g., FI = 8 minutes, FR = 3) we observe an abrupt transition from post-reinforcement pause to high and stable terminal rate. Such performance has characteristics which resemble those seen in simple _____ _____ schedules, as illustrated in the figure. /

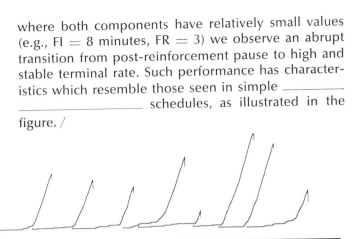

ratio or *fixed ratio*

Increasing the interval size in a Tand FI FR schedule greatly alters performance. The figure shows Tand FI 45 FR 10. Compare these records with those presented in the preceding frame. In addition to the relatively low overall rate, there is a(n) gradual _____● _____ acceleration to an intermediate _____ rate. /

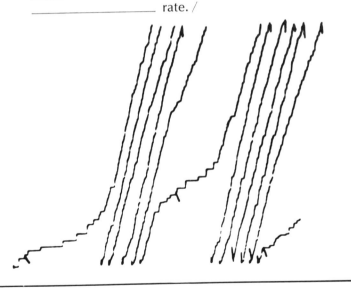

positive
terminal

In the preceding Tand FI 45 FR 10 schedule (unlike the Tand FI 8 FR 3) there (is, is not) an abrupt transition to the terminal rate. /

is not

Finally, performance maintained by a tandem schedule composed of a long FI and small FR produces a variable local rate and intermediate rates that are gradually shifting to a more regular and high running rate. /

The relative values of the two schedules can obviously have profound effects on performance. Addition of a time-out contingency can, similarly, produce major changes in behavior. In this case a TO 15 has been added to the Tand FI 45 FR 10. Notice the overall rate, the very long post-reinforcement pause, and the (more, less) gradual transition to a high and stable terminal rate. /

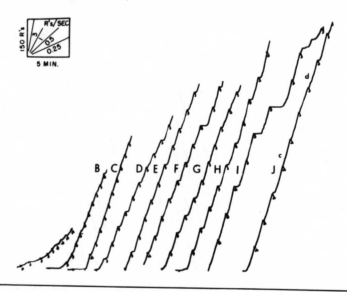

more

Thus, relatively low values of Tand FI FR schedules produce performance resembling _____ schedules. Increasing the relative values of the FI and/or FR components is associated with increased local-rate variability. /

simple

Tand FI FR with long FI and small FR values has an intermediate overall rate, variable local rate, and gradual transition to a moderate terminal rate. /

Tandem FI FRs with short FIs and large FR values have a(n) _____ overall rate due to predominant control by the FR contingency and minimal control by the FI contingency (not shown). /

high

Addition of a TO contingency to a Tand FI FR with long FI and small FR values causes a(n) _____● _____ in overall rate, (long, short) pausing, and (smooth, irregular) transition to a relatively _____ terminal rate. /

increase
long
smooth
high

In the foregoing cases, the conjunction of the FR component and reinforcement brings the performance under the control of a high-rate contingency. Reversing the order of the components to Tand FR FI eliminates the differential reinforcement of _____● _____ rates, but tends to maintain an approximately constant fixed number of responses per reinforcement. /

III-74

Thus, the relation between reinforcement and immediately preceding responses in Tand FR FI schedules will be that of a(n) _____ contingency, where the probability of reinforcement increases with the time since last reinforcement. /

interval

III-75

If the FI component of a Tand FR FI is only a few seconds long, the variation in number of responses from FR segment to FR segment is necessarily slight. /

III-76

The early development of Tand FR FI with moderate to small FRs and very small FIs closely resembles the development of simple FR performance, as shown. /

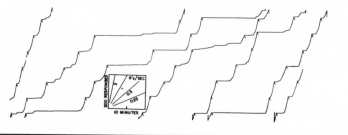

III-77

However, as the ratio is increased to a very high value, performance goes through a progression of changes. The preceding segments show transition states and later performance. /

III-78

Thus, while tandem schedules are often used to reveal stimulus functions in corresponding _____●
_____ schedules, they are, in themselves, of interest in providing information about schedule control. /

Objectives

1 Define a chained schedule of reinforcement.
III-3 to III-6

2 What two kinds of operants may be chained together?
III-7 to III-9

3 What two functions do the stimuli perform in a chain schedule?
III-10 to III-15

4 How would it be possible to establish a conditioned reinforcer without requiring emission of a response? What is the schedule called? What kind of operant is involved?
III-16, also I-15 to I-18

5 What determines the frequency of reinforcement in the components of chained VI schedules?
III-16 to III-21

6 What is the behavioral effect of altering the relative temporal values of the first and second components of a two-component VI chain?
III-19 to III-31

7 What determines the probability of reinforcement on ratio schedules?
III-32

8 How are the reinforcing properties of stimuli associated with FR chain components affected by probability of reinforcement?
III-33 to III-36

9 In a three member chain, which member of the chain is most severely affected by a change in the response requirement in any member of the chain?
III-38 to III-47

10 What are the two main variables which affect the reinforcing properties of the stimuli associated with each member in that chain?
III-16 to III-21, III-32, III-48 to III-50

11 What is a tandem reinforcement schedule?
III-51 and III-52

12 What is the difference between a chain schedule and a tandem schedule?
III-3 to III-6, III-51 to III-54

13 In an experiment where both chained and tandem schedules are used, what variable is being controlled and what variable is being considered?
III-54 and III-55

14 Why are Tandem VR VR and Tandem FR FR considered to be trivial?

III-61

15 What is the difference in the performance characteristics of a tandem FI FR and a Tandem FR FI?

III-62 to III-67, III-69 to III-71, III-73 to III-77

Multiple Reinforcement Schedules

III-79

In both chained and tandem reinforcement schedules, unconditioned reinforcement occurs only on completion of the terminal component. Corresponding to chained and tandem schedules are two schedules, one with discriminative stimuli associated with each component, the other without discriminative stimuli, but *both having unconditioned reinforcement presented at the end of each component.* /

III-80

The reinforcement schedule corresponding to a chained schedule (i.e., with discriminative _____ •
_____ associated with each component but with unconditioned reinforcement presented on completion of each component) is called a *multiple reinforcement schedule.* /

stimuli

III-81

An exception to the foregoing definition of a multiple schedule is when an extinction schedule is one of the components. In such a case a discriminative stimulus is associated with each component, but in the extinction component unconditioned reinforcement (is, is not) forthcoming. /

is not

III-82

The reinforcement schedule corresponding to a tandem schedule (i.e., *without* discriminative stimuli

224

associated with each component, however, with unconditioned reinforcement coming at the end of each component) is called a *mixed reinforcement schedule.* /

In the presence of a green light each 100th response is reinforced, and in the presence of a red light the first response after 10 minutes is reinforced. This would be a(n) _____ FR 100 FI 10 reinforcement schedule. /

multiple

The schedule in the foregoing frame would *not* be a chained schedule because food reinforcement was presented following completion of the _____● _____ component as well as the FI 10. /

FR 100

The behavior of a pole vaulter is maintained by tandem reinforcement contingencies since there is no discrete stimulus change on completion of the run that precedes the jump. Similarly, a monkey that pushes a button a variable number of times to receive a pellet of food in one component and a fixed number of times also leading to food may have no stimuli that indicate which contingencies are in effect. The latter case differs in that an unconditioned reinforcer follows completion of each component. Therefore, the latter would be a(n) _____ reinforcement schedule. /

mixed

Consider the following example of a schedule in which an FR 10 schedule, reinforced by food, is in effect during a red light followed by a FI 1 schedule reinforced by water in the presence of a white light,

225

followed by a VR 50 schedule reinforced by sugar in the presence of a tone. This is an example of a(n) _____ component _____ schedule. /

three
multiple

A three component schedule begins with a tone and a temporal contingency (IRT < 10) leading to an unconditioned negative reinforcer (e.g., shock) if a response does not occur. Following a response or the occurrence of shock a buzzer is presented and 25 responses produce water. Then light onset is correlated with a 5 minute extinction schedule. This is an example of a(n) _____ component _____ schedule of _____ reinforcement, _____ _____ reinforcement, and extinction. /

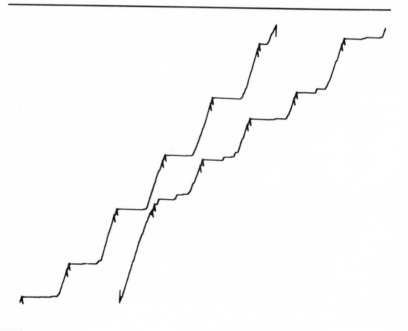

three
multiple
negative
positive

The cumulative record shows terminal performance on a multiple schedule. From these records you might surmise that this is a Mult FI _____ schedule. /

FR

Notice the rather discrete changes from performance characteristic of a ratio contingency to the very long pauses and positive acceleration to running rate of a(n) _____ contingency. /

interval

The extent to which discriminative stimuli control behavior appropriate to a given schedule condition is shown. /

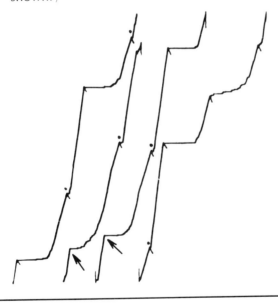

After a history of Mult FI 5 FR 80, the FI light was presented in the middle of ratio runs, as indicated by the arrows. Over successive intrusions of the FI stim-

ulus, the shift to more fixed _____-like performance following stimulus change becomes apparent. /

interval

III-92

Occasionally, responding occurs erratically, with features of both schedules occurring under both stimulus
conditions. One way of reducing such "indiscrimi-
nate" responding is adding a TO contingency. As
indicated in the figures, the initial change produced
by the time out was an overall rate _____. /

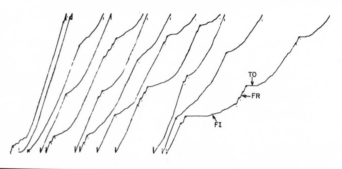

decrease

III-93

While in earlier examples of multiple schedules a
single occurrence of each component was programmed sequentially, in the immediately preceding
example the contingencies of the several components
were in effect for specified durations. Thus, varying
numbers of fixed ratio completions occurred in succession. At the arrow labeled FR 3, completions of
the ratio contingency occurred. This was preceded by
the _____ component and followed by
the _____ component of the multiple
schedule. /

FI
TO

III-94

With longer exposure to the Mult FI FR TO schedule,

228

appropriate properties of each individual schedule returned, generating (less, more) scalloping during FI components and (more, less) abrupt change to ratio performance during FR components. /

more

more

III-95

Prolonged exposure to multiple schedules with components of the same type (e.g., both FRs) but varying in value yield equally discrete performances. /

III-96

The figure shows behavior on Mult FR 60 FR 200, with responding in each component recorded on separate cumulative recorders. The FR 60 component from one recorder is shown at _____; the FR 200 component from the other recorder is shown at _____ _____. /

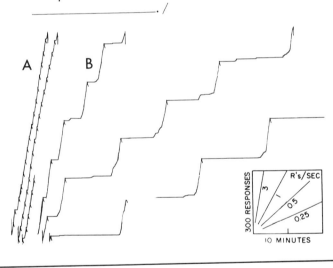

A

15

B

III-97

Similar control can be exercised over interval schedules as well, as revealed by the record of Mult FI 15

FI 2. The FI 2 performance is at _____ and FI _____ performance is at _____. /

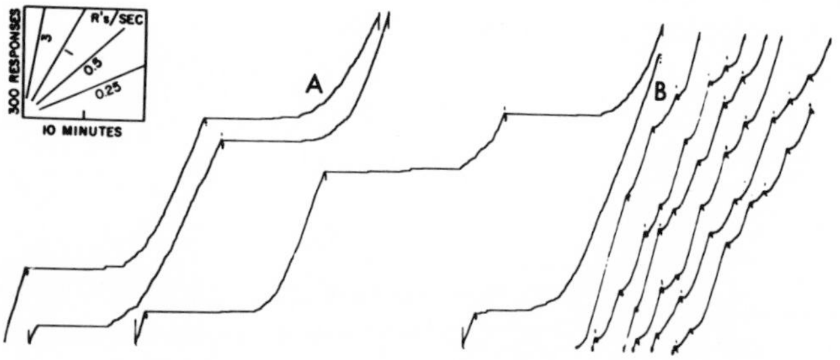

B
15
A

The two foregoing examples each had two components and are therefore called two *ply* schedules. Thus, "ply" refers to the number of _____ in a multiple schedule. /

components

An FR 50 schedule in the presence of a green light, followed by an FR 100 schedule in the presence of an orange light, and then by an FR 500 in the presence of a violet light, with food reinforcement upon completion of each component, is an example of a(n) _____ ply schedule. /

three

It might seem that establishing good stimulus control over three such similar schedules would be very difficult, if not unlikely. The figure shows very good control over a Mult FR 50 FR 250 FI 2 FI 11 schedule, which is a(n) _____ ply schedule. /

230

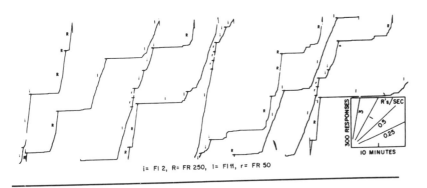

i= FI 2, R= FR 250, I= FI ff, r= FR 50

four

An example of a seven ply multiple schedule that includes the following components is shown (four component records shown): (1) free-operant avoidance, (2) discriminated avoidance, (3) time out, (4) IRT > 10 sec, (5) CRF, (6) FR 50, and (7) complex discrimination on CRF. /

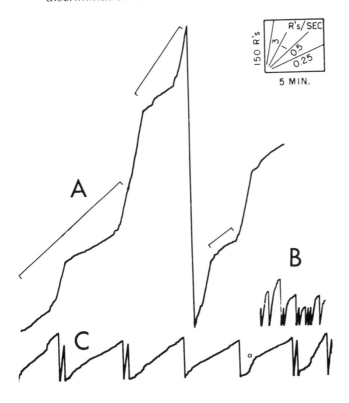

To a remarkable degree, performance during the ratio, IRT > 10 sec, and avoidance components resemble that produced using simple schedules. It thus appears possible to maintain good stimulus and ___●
_____ control for sustained periods, using multiple scheduling. /

schedule

As might be imagined, behavior in the respective components of multiple schedules is not always independent of other components. A change in the rate of responding during the presentation of one stimulus, brought about by changing the schedule associated with another stimulus, is called *interaction*. /

If, for example, performance is stabilized on Mult VI 1 VI 2, and the schedule during the stimulus for VI 2 is changed to extinction, the rate during the stimulus for VI 1 will tend to increase. Such a change has been called a *behavioral contrast*, which is an example of a(n) _____. /

interaction

Behavioral contrast can most readily be studied in two ply multiple schedules, where the complexity of the possible interactions is minimized. /

When a reinforced component is maintained at the same value while a second component is placed on extinction (as in the preceding example), response rate in the reinforced component increases. This is called a *positive contrast*. /

An animal stabilized on Mult VR 5 VR 50 is shifted to Mult VR 5 EXT. We would expect the rate in the

VR 5 component to _____. This would be an example of a(n) _____ contrast. /

increase
positive

III-108

A decrease in responding occurs when the schedule in the other component is changed from extinction to one of reinforcement. Such a decrease is called a *negative contrast*. /

III-109

An animal is trained on Mult VI 10 EXT, then shifted to Mult VI 10 VI 2. The response rate during the VI 10 component will tend to _____. This would be an example of a(n) _____ contrast. /

decrease
negative

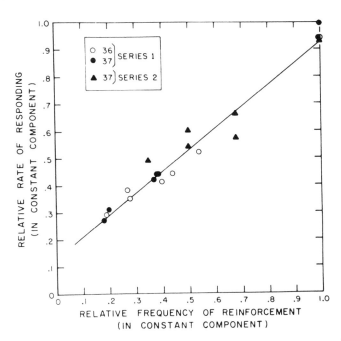

Such positive and negative contrasts are not limited to schedules involving an extinction component. Indeed, it seems that the relative rate of responding varies linearly with the frequency of reinforcement in a given component (relative to the second component). The figure on the preceding page illustrates the relation between relative response rate and relative frequency of reinforcement during the constant VI component of a Mult VI FR schedule. /

As the value of the FR component increases, a smaller proportion of the total reinforcements are in this component and a larger proportion are in the VI component. That is, the relative frequency of reinforcement increases in the VI component. /

Thus, as the frequency of reinforcement during the FR component decreases, the relative rate during the VI component _____. /

increases

Conversely, as the frequency of reinforcement during the FR component increases, the relative rate during the VI component _____. This would be an illustration of a(n) _____. /

decreases
negative contrast

Mixed Reinforcement Schedules

In the foregoing discussion different discriminative stimuli were presented during each component of a schedule, and unconditioned reinforcement was forthcoming on completion of each component. In the following schedule FI 5 performance is reinforced with food, followed by a component in which 50

234

response (FR 50) avoids shock presentation. /

III-115

This schedule differs from the preceding schedules in that it lacks the discriminative stimuli associated with each component. It would therefore be a(n) _____● _____ reinforcement schedule. /

mixed

III-116

The schedule in the preceding frame would be abbreviated Mix _____ _____. /

FI 15 FR 50

III-117

In comparing mixed and multiple schedules, it should be obvious that multiple schedules will be under stimulus control, whereas mixed schedules will be exclusively under _____ control. /

schedule

III-118

Because of the formal similarity of chained and multiple schedules, with the exception of reinforcement after each component in the latter schedule, chained schedules are sometimes used to evaluate the conditioned reinforcing properties of stimuli in _____● _____ schedules. /

multiple

III-119

Consider a schedule composed of the following components:
1. FR 25   tone   food
2. FI 5   light   water
3. FR 100   buzzer   fruit /

III-120

From the foregoing description of the schedule, which

235

of the cumulative records shown would be generated by these contingencies? _____ /

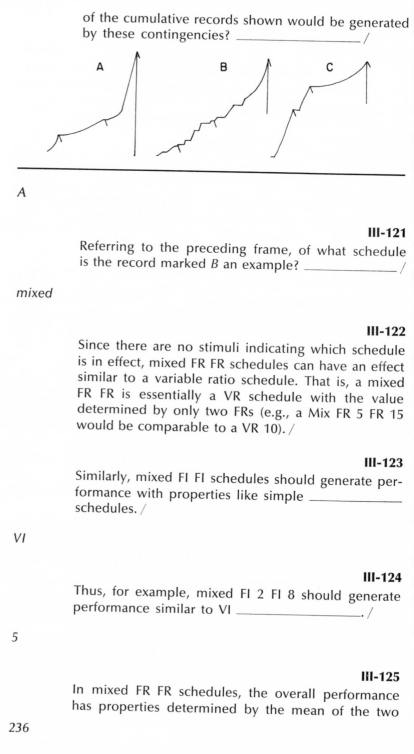

A

Referring to the preceding frame, of what schedule is the record marked *B* an example? _____ /

mixed

Since there are no stimuli indicating which schedule is in effect, mixed FR FR schedules can have an effect similar to a variable ratio schedule. That is, a mixed FR FR is essentially a VR schedule with the value determined by only two FRs (e.g., a Mix FR 5 FR 15 would be comparable to a VR 10). /

Similarly, mixed FI FI schedules should generate performance with properties like simple _____ schedules. /

VI

Thus, for example, mixed FI 2 FI 8 should generate performance similar to VI _____. /

5

In mixed FR FR schedules, the overall performance has properties determined by the mean of the two ratios, although stabilized Mix FR FR reveals schedule control of individual schedules as well. /

III-126

Thus, whether pausing appears depends on the mean of the two _____ and the proportions with which they are used in the program. /

ratios

III-127

In a Mix FR 10 FR 90, the overall performance will not only depend on the _____ of the two ratios (which is _____ in this case), but will also be determined by the proportion of FR 10 and FR 90 units. /

mean or *average*
50

III-128

For example, a bird on Mix FR 60 FR 360, with two FR 360 units for every ten FR 60 units, paused little or not at all. (A) When the proportion of the two FRs was changed to nine FR 60 units for every three FR 360 units, pausing appeared (B), as shown in the figure. /

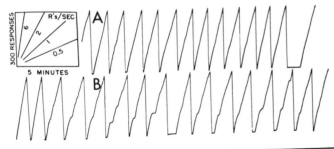

III-129

Compare the next example, which shows early performance on Mix FR FR with frequent overlap of performance appropriate to one schedule into the other schedule's programmed contingency. Variability in ratio runs is substantial. /

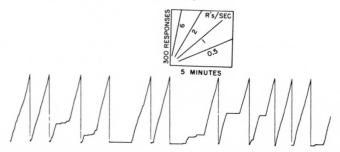

III-130

However, after Mix FR FR has stabilized, a pattern emerges in which the animal emits a run of responses approximately equal to the smaller ratio size, pauses, then emits another run appropriate to the larger ratio size. Such an initial run and pause is called *priming* and will persist briefly in the absence of reinforcement. /

III-131

Priming is one of the indications that performance is coming under good schedule control. However, the absence of discriminative stimuli might lead one to expect schedule control of performance on mixed schedules to be relatively weak. The figure shows transition from Mix FR 50 FR 240 (*A*) to Mult FR 50 FR 240 (*B*). Notice the marked pausing following schedule change, producing a(n) _____ overall rate. /

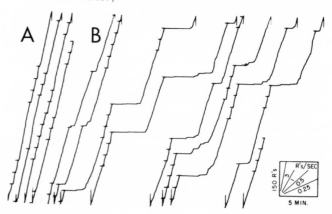

238

diminished or
  decreased

III-132

If animals are first trained on Mult FR 120 FR 5, then changed to mixed schedules of the same value, the overall rate is expected to _____. /

increase

III-133

One can therefore conclude that _____ schedules are more readily maintained at high overall rates than _____ schedules, where comparable schedule values are employed. /

mixed
multiple

III-134

In comparing Mix FI FI (as seen in the figure) with Mix FR FR discussed earlier, note the low overall rate of the FI performance, the marked irregularity, and variable local rate. /

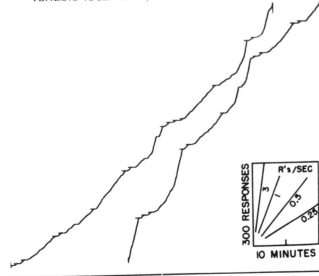

III-135

Instead of characteristic FI scallops, there are deep

239

scallops and (brief, no) pausing. /

brief

III-136
The preceding figure of Mix FI FI shows particularly well the variable local rate and _____ overall rate. /

low

III-137
The relative inadequacy of schedule control with the Mix FI FI can be eliminated by adding an exteroceptive stimulus, referred to earlier in discussing simple FI schedules as a(n) _____ ___●
_____. /

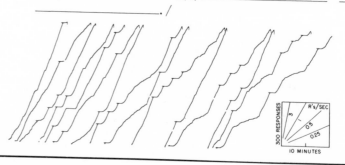

added clock

III-138
Notice that scalloping has become (shallower, deeper) and that overall rates are (lower, higher). /

deeper
higher

III-139
Combining FIs and FRs in mixed schedules creates more stable performance than Mix FI FI but less schedule control of performance than Mix FR FR. /

III-140
Transition to Mix FI FR from Mult FI FR produces

240

changes comparable to the previously discussed change from Mix to Mult FR FR. The transition records reveal (brief, extended) pauses and (slight, considerable) variability of local rate. /

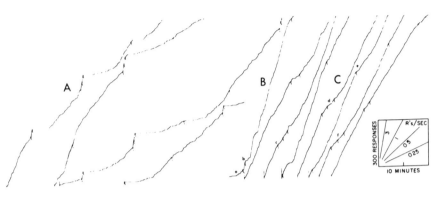

extended

considerable

After extended training on mixed FI FR schedules, stabilized performance with characteristics of individual components emerges. /

In our earlier discussion of fixed ratio schedules, it was pointed out that the term "post-reinforcement pause" is somewhat a misnomer. Comparisons of performance generated by multiple and mixed FR FR schedules makes this clearer. /

These records show performance by a rat on randomized mixed FR 20 FR 40 (left) and multiple FR 20 FR 40 (right). In the mixed schedule there are no discriminative stimuli indicating which component was in effect, while in the multiple schedule, colored lights indicated which component was active. /

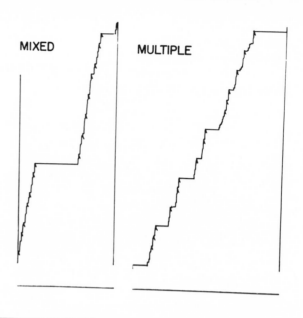

MIXED   MULTIPLE

Since no _____ stimulus was present during the mixed schedule, any pausing that occurred following a given reinforcement could not be due to the value of the next component (i.e., there was no indication whether it would be FR 20 or FR 40). /

discriminative

Notice that the two long pauses occur before short ratios, although there was little pausing otherwise. /

In the multiple schedule, on the other hand, distinctive stimuli indicated which component was in effect following reinforcement. Hence pausing could be due to the size of the ratio just completed or to the size of the ratio currently in effect. /

Notice that all long pauses occurred *before* long ratios regardless of the ratio just completed. Hence it would be more accurate to describe them as pre-

ratio pauses rather than post-_____
pauses. /

reinforcement

III-148

A final type of sequential reinforcement schedule is distinguished by inserting or interpolating a simple schedule into a second "background" schedule, which is also a simple schedule. Such a schedule is called an *interpolated* (abbreviated *interpol*) reinforcement schedule. /

III-149

A fixed-interval 10-minute (FI 10) background schedule is interrupted for 10 reinforcements on an FR 50 schedule, then the FI 10 schedule resumes. The FR 50 is _____ on the background schedule. This schedule is written as FI 10 _____ FR 50. /

interpolated
Interpol

III-150

Interpolated schedules have no discriminative stimuli associated with each component; however, reinforcement is forthcoming during both the background schedule and the interpolated schedule. Thus, an interpolated schedule can be thought of as a special case of a(n) _____ reinforcement schedule. /

mixed

III-151

As with other mixed schedules, data of particular interest include the changeover to the interpolated schedule, the development of performance on the interpolated schedule, and the changeover back to the background schedule. The following record of FI 5 interpol FR 40 illustrates the insertion of _____●

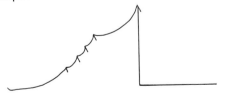

FR 40
FI 5

CONCURRENT REINFORCEMENT
SCHEDULES (OPTIONS)

III-152

Up to this point we have limited our discussion to simple operants or serial sequences of operants. Operants may as well be arranged in parallel or *concurrently*. Such schedules have come to be called concurrent reinforcement schedules. /

III-153

Another name for concurrent reinforcement schedules is *options*. In an option at least two individual operants are programmed to be in effect. /

III-154

A rat can press a lever to receive food pellets on an FR 10 and concurrently pull a nearby chain on an FI 2 leading to water reinforcement. Both contingencies are in effect at all times and are totally independent. This is called a *reversible option* and can be designated *Conc* FR 10 FI 2. /

III-155

If the program were changed in the foregoing case, so the first response on the lever terminated the animal's opportunity to receive water reinforcement until the FR 10 for food had been completed, the schedule would be called a *nonreversible option*. Nonreversible options are also examples of _____•
_____ reinforcement schedules. /

concurrent

III-156

A monkey is provided with two schedules: FR 100 on one lever produces food, and water reinforcement is obtained on a VI 10 contingent on a chain pull. If the first lever press precludes the possibility of obtaining water until the 100th lever press, this would be called a(n) _____ option. /

nonreversible

244

If in the foregoing case effective responses could be emitted on either manipulation simultaneously or in alternation this would be called a reversible option. In that case, the organism could work toward satisfying the FR 100 and VI 10 contingencies (independently, dependently) _____ or _____●
_____. /

independently
concurrently (or)
 simultaneously

Chickens were trained on a nonreversible option composed of FR schedules for food, water, and mirror reinforcement. By progressively increasing the values of the ratios over sessions, it was possible to assess the effectiveness of these three reinforcers. The graph illustrates this relationship. From the data it seems that _____ is the most effective reinforcer. /

food

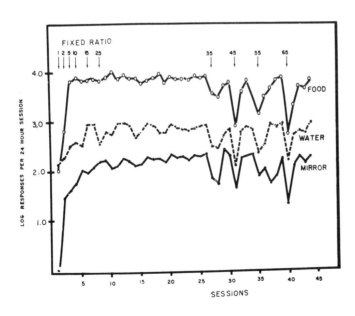

Options, or _____ operants, must be topographically compatible to maximize independence of two operants. For example, pressing a button with the left hand and pulling a chain with the right hand are compatible if the manipulanda are in close proximity. /

concurrent

In other cases, although it might appear on the surface that two operants are compatible, they are in fact mutually exclusive. Consider a two key option in the pigeon. Although the keys are close together, the bird is unable to peck both keys at precisely the same time. Therefore, the two operants are _____●
_____. /

incompatible

Independence of reversible options is difficult to establish. When two responses occur simultaneously, the consequences of one necessarily have an effect on both. For example, if a button is pressed at the same moment a chain pull leads to food reinforcement, the button press is reinforced as well as the chain pull. Behavior which is inadvertently reinforced in this way was called _____ behavior earlier in the program. /

superstitious

The accidental correlation of an operant with reinforcement programmed for a second operant is called concurrent _____. /

superstition

246

The cumulative records shown illustrate interaction between components of a two member option. Pigeons had been conditioned on a VI 1-minute schedule on both keys but now were placed on extinction of one key, with the second key remaining on VI 1. /

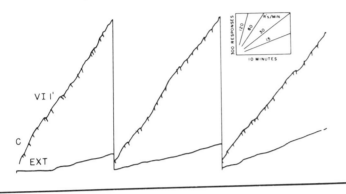

There are a substantial number of pecks on the "extinction" key, despite the fact that no explicit contingency exists between pecks on that key and reinforcement. It would appear that some of the pecks on the EXT key are occasionally being followed by a response to the VI 1 key (called a changeover response), producing reinforcement. This would be an example of _____ superstition. /

concurrent

One technique for producing a separation of the contingencies for two operants is to impose a delay between emission of one operant and the subsequent reinforcement of a second response. For example, in the preceding instance one might program a 1-second-delay requirement that a response on the extinction key followed by a VI key response could be reinforced only if a 1-second delay had elapsed between the two responses. Such a *delay* between the *changeover* response and the possibility of reinforcement is called a *changeover delay.* /

The cumulative record shows the effect on the extinction component of imposing a 1-second *change-over delay*, abbreviated _____, on the concurrent VI 1 EXT schedule. /

COD

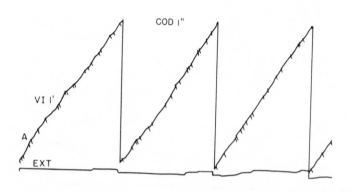

The separation between the changeover response and reinforcement decreases the likelihood of ___●
_____ reinforcement. /

superstitious or
 accidental

Among the little-understood features of concurrent VI schedules is what has been called "matching" [i.e., response rate is correlated with (matches) reinforcement frequency]. This refers to the fact that the number of responses emitted under appropriate stimulus conditions on each key of a two-member concurrent VI schedule varies inversely with the value of the VIs. /

Or, stated another way, the relative time spent in the presence of a given key color in a two member concurrent VI schedule varies inversely with the ___●
_____ of the interval. /

size or *value*

Since the value of the schedule is inversely proportional to the reinforcement density in a VI schedule,
one might suppose that the time in each component
of a concurrent VI schedule would vary directly with
the relative reinforcement density. The figure shows
that, indeed, this is the case. /

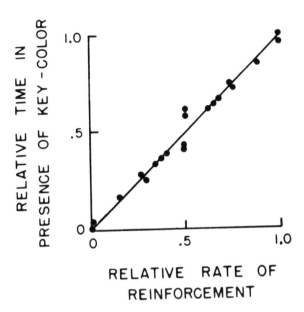

RELATIVE RATE OF
REINFORCEMENT

Thus, while the exact mechanism is not understood,
it seems that time in a given component of a concurrent VI schedule varies directly with the _____
_____ _____ _____
_____ . /

density of
reinforcement

The cumulative record on the following page shows
interaction between fixed interval and fixed ratio components in a two-member reversible option (Conc FR
100 FI 5 min). /

Early in the FI 5 the FR 100 continues at a high rate, but pausing becomes evident toward the end of the 5 minute interval as responding changes over to the FI key. /

Options may involve any of the contingencies or consequences discussed earlier. These include all the simple reinforcement schedules, behavior-independent _____, temporal contingencies, and negative operants. /

contingencies

One special type of reversible option is a two member option, which necessarily involves interval and ratio contingencies. Such an option is called an *alternative reinforcement* schedule and will be discussed at greater length in Section IV. /

All the options described thus far have involved separate operanda for each operant. Operants can also be programmed concurrently on a single operandum. Such contingencies are called *conjoint* schedules, to distinguish them from those multiple operandum schedules previously designated as _____ operants or options. /

concurrent
250

Monkeys were trained to press one lever on an FR 100 schedule for food and to press a second lever on a free-operant avoidance schedule to avoid shock. Since the two schedules were in effect at the same time, this would be called a(n) _____ schedule. /

concurrent

The figure presents sample cumulative records of performance generated by the foregoing schedule. Notice that behavior maintained by each reinforcer is appropriate to the individual contingencies and reflects little interaction between the schedules. /

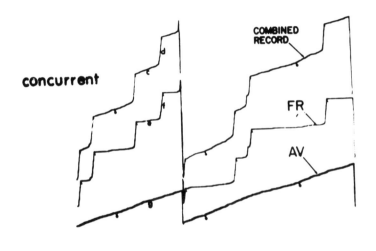

Now the same experiment is run and programmed identically except only one manipulandum serves both schedules. The figure illustrates behavior maintained on the single operandum by these concurrent contingencies. /

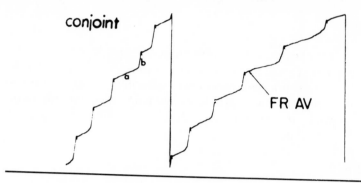

conjoint

FR AV

III-180

The combined record on the two-response (_____•
_____ schedule) resembles the single-
response record in the _____ schedule
situation. /

concurrent

conjoint

III-181

Thus, the features of the two schedules which are
separated by the _____ schedules are
combined by the _____ schedule. The
value of the concurrent schedule is in separating interactions between concurrent contingencies. /

concurrent

conjoint

Objectives

1 What is a multiple schedule?
  III-80 and III-81
2 What is the relationship between the following two groups
  of schedules: chained and tandem schedules and mixed and
  multiple schedules?
  III-79 to III-82, III-3 to III-6, III-51 to III-54
3 Give an example of a three component multiple schedule
  which includes a temporal contingency, a ratio contingency,
  and an extinction component.
  III-87
4 In a multiple FR FR schedule, when features of both schedules occur under both stimulus conditions, what is one way
  of improving discrimination of the different schedules?
  Does the improved schedule control take place immediately
  or over a period of time?
  III-92 to III-94

5 To what does the term "ply" refer when discussing multiple schedules?
III-98 and III-99

6 Define schedule interaction.
III-103 to III-108

7 What is behavioral contrast?
III-104 and III-105, III-110

8 Give an example of a schedule interaction that would cause a positive behavioral contrast.
III-106 and III-107, III-110

9 Give an example of a schedule interaction that would cause negative behavioral contrast.
III-108 and III-109, III-113

10 What is a mixed schedule?
III-114 to III-116

11 Performance under which schedule, multiple or mixed, is more likely to be under stimulus control and under which will schedule control be most important?
III-117

12 A mixed FR FR schedule resembles what simple schedule?
III-122

13 A mixed FI FI schedule resembles what simple schedule?
III-123 and III-124

14 In a mixed FI FI or mixed FR FR, what parameter of the two schedules determines the overall performance?
III-125

15 Pausing sometimes develops in mixed schedules. What two factors determine how much pausing there is?
III-126 to III-128

16 What is priming?
III-129 and III-130

17 What quality of control does priming indicate?
III-131

18 Which schedules, mixed or multiple, are most likely to maintain high overall rates if comparable schedule values are employed?
III-133

19 What is the effect on the overall performance if there is a transition from a mixed FI FI to a multiple FI FI?
III-136 to III-138

20 What is an interpolated schedule?
III-148 to III-150

21 Define concurrent schedules. What is another name for concurrent reinforcement schedules?

III-152 and III-153

22 What is the difference between reversible and nonreversible options?

III-154 to III-156

23 To assess the strength of reinforcers in a three member nonreversible option, what schedule could be applied to each of the members to assess its strength?

III-158

24 Options or concurrent operants must be topographically compatible, and yet topographical compatibility may level to behavioral incompatibility. Why?

III-159 to III-162, III-165

25 What is one type of interaction which may occur under concurrent operants?

III-162 to III-164 (interaction, see III-103 to III-108)

26 What procedure may be used to avoid accidental reinforcement in a concurrent schedule?

III-165

27 When concurrent VI schedules are used, what determines the time spent in each of the components?

III-166 to III-171

28 What is a conjoint schedule?

III-176

29 What is the value of a concurrent schedule over a conjoint schedule?

III-181

References

III-23 Response output per reinforcement as a function of mean VI in the second component of a two component chain.

Findley, J. D., "An Experimental Outline for Building and Exploring Multi-operant Behavior Repertoires." *Journal of the Experimental Analysis of Behavior, 5,* No. 1 (Jan., 1962), 113; Fig. 5, p. 128.

III-27 Rate as a function of mean VI in the first component of a two-component chain.

Findley, J. D., "An Experimental Outline for Building and Exploring Multi-operant Behavior Repertoires." *Journal of the Experimental Analysis of Behavior, 5,* No. 1 (Jan., 1962), 113; Fig. 6, p. 128

III-29 Cumulative-record segments of performance on a two-component chain, VI schedule.

255

multiple FI FR to mixed FI FR, pigeon.

III-151 Stylized curve of performance on FI 5 interpolated FR 460 schedule.

III-158 Relationship between effectiveness of three reinforcers, fighting cock.

Thompson, T. T., "Visual Reinforcement in Fighting Cocks." *Journal of the Experimental Analysis of Behavior*, 7, No. 1 (Jan., 1964), 45–49; Fig. 1, p. 47.

III-163 Cumulative record of interaction between two components of a two member option.

Catania, A. C., "Concurrent Operants" in *Operant Behavior: Areas of Research and Application*, W. K. Honig, ed. New York, Appleton-Century-Crofts, 1966; Fig. 1, p. 217.

III-166 Cumulative record of concurrent schedule with two members and COD.

Catania, A. C., "Concurrent Operants" in *Operant Behavior: Areas of Research and Application*; Fig. 2.

III-170 Effect of reinforcement rate on time spent in compartment of concurrent schedule.

Catania, A. C., "Concurrent Operants" in *Operant Behavior: Areas of Research and Application*; Fig. 9, p. 242.

III-172 Catania, A. C., "Concurrent Operants" in *Operant Behavior: Areas of Research and Application*; Fig. 4.

III-178 Cumulative-record segments of performance generated by concurrent AV FR schedule.

Catania, A. C., Deegan, J. F., and Cook, L., "Concurrent Fixed ratio and Avoidance Responding in the Squirrel Monkey." *Journal of the Experimental Analysis of Behavior*, 9, No. 3 (May, 1966) 227–232; Fig. 1, p. 229.

III-179 Cumulative-record segments of performance generated by conjoint AV FR schedule.

Catania, A. C., Deegan, J. F., and Cook, L., "Concurrent Fixed ratio and Avoidance Responding in the Squirrel Monkey." *Journal of the Experimental Analysis of Behavior*, 9, No. 3 (May, 1966), 227–232.

Section IV

COMPLEX REINFORCEMENT SCHEDULES

SCHEDULES WITH CONSTANT RATIO AND INTERVAL CONTINGENCIES

IV-1

Reinforcement schedules which involve both ratio and interval contingencies on the same operandum are called *complex reinforcement schedules*. There are two main subtypes of complex schedules: (1) schedules in which the values of ratio and interval contingencies are fixed, independent of behavior, and (2) schedules in which the value of ratio or interval values vary as a function of previous behavior. /

IV-2

Reinforcement schedules in which ratios and/or intervals remain fixed regardless of preceding behavior include *conjunctive reinforcement schedules* and *alternative reinforcement schedules*. Both are examples of _____ schedules. /

complex

Conjunctive Reinforcement Schedules

IV-3

In a conjunctive (*Conj*) schedule, both a ratio and an interval requirement must be satisfied before reinforcement is forthcoming. An animal that will be reinforced following the emission of 50 responses *and* after 1 minute has elapsed is on a *Conj* _____●
_____ _____ schedule. /

258

IV-4

In the preceding Conj FI 1 FR 50 schedule, the length of the FI and the value of the FR remained _____● _____ regardless of the subject's preceding behavior. /

fixed or *constant*

IV-5

The graphs illustrate the conditions for reinforcement on FI, FR, and Conj FI FR schedules. Notice that in the FI curve the number of responses before the fixed interval has elapsed varies, but only one reinforcement is obtained. Conversely, on a FR schedule, the length of time to complete 50 responses may vary, but only one reinforcement is obtained. Depending on the response rate, more than 50 responses may be emitted prior to reinforcement or more than the fixed interval in a Conj FI 1 FR 50 schedule. /

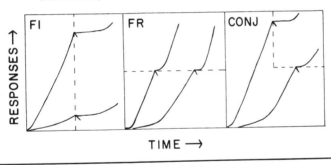

IV-6

Performance in such a conjunctive schedule should reflect an interaction of ratio and interval contingencies, varying with the values of the two sets of contingencies. /

IV-7

Pigeons trained on a FI 15-minute schedule were subsequently switched to Conj FI 15 FR, where the value of the ratio contingency was varied from FR 1,

259

through intermediate values, to FR 240. The figure shows the relation between response rate and ratio size for two subjects. /

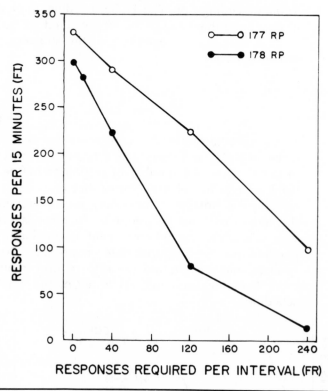

IV-8
There is a(n) (direct, inverse) relation between FR size and response rate. /

inverse

IV-9
Indeed, the response rates at all values above FR 1 (i.e, a simple FI 15 schedule) are (higher, lower) than the rate for simple FI 15. /

lower

IV-10
Thus, the addition of a contingency of number of re-

sponses to a fixed interval schedule has the effect of (decreasing, increasing) overall rate, proportional to the response requirement. /

decreasing

IV-11

This rate diminishing effect of the conjunctive ratio contingency is puzzling until the consequences of adding a response-number requirement are carefully considered. If the average number of responses per interval in a simple FI 15 schedule equals 10, it would seem that a Conj FI 15 FR 10 should be equivalent to an FI 15. In fact, the number of responses per interval in a simple schedule will vary from 1 to 50. Thus, even if the *average* number of responses per FI 15 is 10, many FI 15 intervals elapse with fewer than 10 responses. /

IV-12

When very few responses have occurred during an FI, the likelihood that the next response will be reinforced will be high, since a greater amount of time has elapsed in the interval. /

IV-13

Thus, low response rates are associated with high probability of reinforcements, while high response rates are associated with _____ probability of reinforcement in an FI schedule. /

low

IV-14

Since the overall response rate is known to vary directly with reinforcement probability, one would expect higher response requirements (which reduce reinforcement probability) to (increase, decrease) the response rate. /

decrease

Thus, the inverse relation between FR value and re-sponse rate in conjunctive schedules may be attrib-utable to the fact that high response rates (increase, decrease) the probability of reinforcement. /

decrease

The sample cumulative records comparing FI 15 TO 5 with Conj FI 15 FR 40, TO 5, reveal that the pattern of responding is affected as well as _____ rate. /

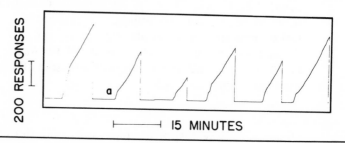

overall

Reinforcement is most probable following pauses with FI contingencies; there is a greater tendency for low rates toward the end of a given fixed interval period since the fixed ratio performance appears early in the interval (relatively high rates). /

Thus, in conjunctive FI FR schedules, increasing the response requirement produces a(n) (increment, de-crement) in overall response rate and changes the pattern of responding to an early fixed _____ ●
_____-like pattern to a later fixed ____●
_____-like pattern. /

decrement
ratio
interval
262

These changes in overall rate and pattern of Conj FI FR are probably attributable to the increased probability of reinforcement at relatively _____ rates during the latter part of FI intervals and the fact that large numbers of responses are associated with _____ reinforcement probability in FI schedules. /

low

low

Alternative Reinforcement Schedules

IV-20

The other type of schedule in which the values of a fixed ratio and fixed interval remain constant regardless of the organism's behavior is an *alternative (Alt) reinforcement schedule.* Such a schedule would be classified as a (simple, compound, complex) reinforcement schedule. /

complex

IV-21

In an alternative reinforcement schedule, reinforcement is forthcoming on completion of either a ratio or interval contingency, whichever is satisfied first. Thus, when an animal is reinforced following the 100th response, or the first response after 2 minutes, whichever comes first, it is known as an Alt _____●
_____ _____ schedule. /

FR 100 FI 2

IV-22

The graph shows the conditions under which responding will be reinforced on an Alt FR 100 FI 2 reinforcement schedule. Compare this graph with that for Conj FR 100 FI 2. /

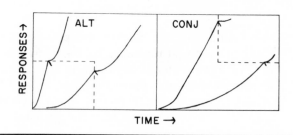

As indicated earlier, an alternative reinforcement schedule is a special type of reversible option in which one contingency is necessarily a ratio and the other necessarily a(n) _____. /

interval

SCHEDULES IN WHICH REINFORCEMENT IS CONTINGENT ON VARYING RATIO AND INTERVAL CONTINGENCIES

IV-24

The number of responses or temporal requirements for reinforcement vary as a function of the subject's past performance. Such contingencies for reinforcement are an example of _____ reinforcement scheduling. /

complex

Adjusting Reinforcement Schedules

IV-25

For example, the number of responses required for reinforcement might increase each time the subject completes an FR in less than 30 seconds. This is an example of an *adjusting (Adj) reinforcement schedule*. /

264

Every time the response rate during a given interval exceeds a specified level, the mean value of a variable ratio schedule increases by 10 percent. This is an example of a(n) _____ reinforcement schedule, abbreviated _____. /

adjusting
Adj

The record shown illustrates performance over a session. If an IRT occurred exceeding 25 seconds, the size of the next ratio was decreased by 5 responses; each time the IRT is less than 25 seconds, the size of the next ratio is increased by 5 responses. This is an example of a(n) _____ schedule, with step size (ratio change value) _____ for pausing 25 seconds or longer. /

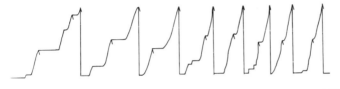

adjusting
5

Over the course of the session in the preceding record, the primary effect was on pause duration, not running rate. Thus, in an adjusting ratio schedule there is (increased, decreased) pausing and unchanged running rate. /

decreased

In another experiment FR size could vary from 10 to 1000, depending on the length of the preceding post-reinforcement pause. The ratio increased whenever two successive IRTs were shorter than a given value, and the response requirement decreased whenever two successive IRTs were longer than a given value. Thus, if the pause length remained within a defined range, the response requirement (increased, was unchanged, decreased). /

was unchanged

The cumulative records show responding with minimum IRTs of 1, 2, 4, 8, and 15 minutes, with the ratio beginning at FR 10. Notice that the response requirements increased rapidly early in the session until a relatively large response requirement was in effect. It appears that the fixed ratio size varies directly with the required _____. /

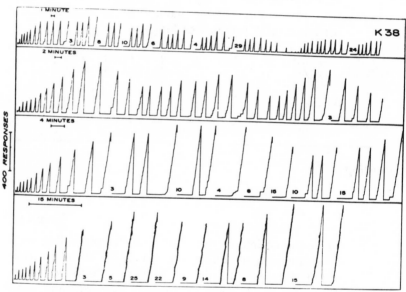

IRTs or inter-response
times

IV-31

The figure shows mean FR values at required pause times 1, 2, 4, 8, and 15 minutes. Notice the direct relation between mean fixed ratio and_____. /

266

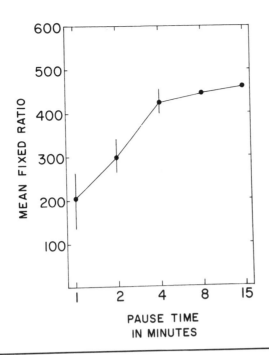

PAUSE TIME
IN MINUTES

pausing

Adjusting schedules are not limited to positive reinforcement contingencies. For example, contingencies
can be programmed so that an animal accumulates
5 seconds of safe time from a shock each time a lever
is pressed. Such contingencies maintain a stable rate
of responding, since the probability of receiving a
shock is related to the amount of time elapsed since
the last response. /

In the foregoing _____ avoidance schedule, the higher the response rate, the longer the
period until the next shock is forthcoming. Thus, the
probability of reinforcement varies as a function of
elapsed time and _____
_____ _____. /

adjusting
number of responses or
response rate

267

Interlocking Reinforcement Schedules

IV-34

In an *adjusting* ratio schedule, the size of each successive ratio is determined by some characteristic of performance since the last reinforcement (e.g., an IRT longer than 25 seconds). In an *interlocking (Int) reinforcement schedule,* the number of responses required per reinforcement is a function of time since the preceding reinforcement; conversely, the time to reinforcement varies as a function of response rate. /

IV-35

Interlocking schedules may be increasing or decreasing; that is, the number of responses required for reinforcement may increase or decrease with elapsed _____ since the preceding reinforcement. /

time

IV-36

The two parameters defining an interlocking schedule are the response requirement and temporal requirements. At the beginning of each interval the time base $= 0$, and the response base equals the maximum fixed ratio. /

IV-37

In the simplest case the number of responses decreases linearly with elapsed time. This relation is summarized in the diagrams of fixed ratio, interlocking and fixed interval schedules shown. /

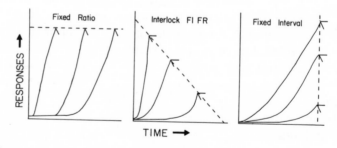

As the amount of time elapsed since the last reinforcement increases along the time base, reinforcement frequency shifts from being primarily
contingent on response _____ to being
primarily dependent on elapsed _____. /

rate
time

Thus, interlocking schedules might be expected to
generate performance whose features are intermediate between _____ _____
and _____ _____
schedules. /

fixed interval
fixed ratio (either order)

In the cumulative records shown, baselines of simple
FR 36 (A) and FI 2 (B) are presented. Notice the characteristic pause and run performance in the _____●
_____ schedule, with the more gradual
scalloped performance in the _____
schedule. /

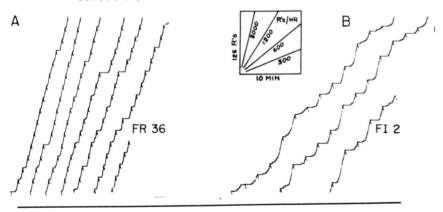

ratio
interval

The figure shows transition from FR 36 to Int FI 2

FR 36. The addition of the fixed interval requirement produces an overall rate decrease, and stabilized performance is ratio-like with long pauses. /

INT FI 2 FR 36

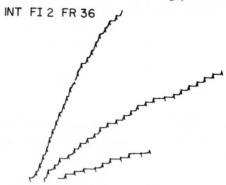

IV-42

By varying the values of the two components, closer approximations to fixed interval performance can be produced. The following records are for another animal on an Int FI 4 FR 72 schedule. /

INT FI 4 FR 72

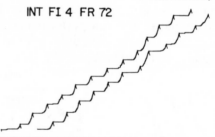

IV-43

Thus, interlocking schedules reveal features intermediate between simple _____ _____●
_____ and simple _____
_____ schedules. /

fixed interval
fixed ratio (either order)

IV-44

An illustration of the sensitivity of the schedule, particularly with respect to the dual-schedule control, involved training rats on an Int FI FR, then administering a hypnotic drug (pentobarbital). The records show the baseline (top segment), followed by the performance over the next 3 hours following drug injection (5 mg/kg) (beginning with the bottom segment). /

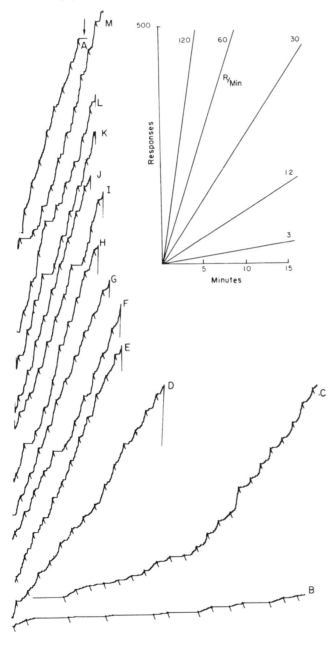

IV-45

The initial effect is an overall ________________ in response rate, with performance resembling neither FI nor FR. As lever pressing gradually returned, shallow scallops changing into deeper scallops, revealing control by the ________________ contingencies, first reappears. Subsequently, a somewhat grainy ________________-like performance emerges, with short pauses and high running rates. /

decrease

FI

ratio

Objectives

1 What is a complex reinforcement schedule?
IV-1 and IV-2

2 What is a conjunctive schedule?
IV-2 and IV-3

3 What are the two main subtypes of complex schedule and what are the distinguishing features?
IV-1 to IV-3, IV-20 and IV-21

4 In a conjunctive schedule, what is the relationship between response rate and FR size?
IV-7 to IV-8

5 Since overall response rate is known to vary directly with reinforcement probability, you would expect higher response requirements to (increase or decrease) response rate.
IV-13 to IV-15

6 In conjunctive schedules, what is the overall response pattern?
IV-17 to IV-19

7 What is an alternative reinforcement schedule?
IV-20 and IV-21, IV-23

8 Is a conjunctive schedule similar to a reversible option or an irreversible option?
IV-23 (reversible options III-148 to III-150)

9 What is an adjusting schedule?
IV-24 to IV-26

10 In an adjusting ratio schedule, is the effect of the "adjusting" contingency observed on the pausing or on the running rate?
IV-27 and IV-28

11 In an adjusting ratio schedule where there is a minimum

pause time, what dependent variable varies directly with the required pause time?
IV-30

12 What is an interlocking schedule?
IV-34

13 What are the two parameters defining an interlocking schedule?
IV-36

14 Toward the end of the interval interlocking schedule, reinforcement shifts from being primarily contingent on responses to being primarily dependent on time. Discuss.
IV-36 to IV-38

15 What is the characteristic performance of interlocking schedules?
IV-39 to IV-44

References

IV-5 Contingencies of FI, FR, and conjoint FIFR schedules.

IV-7 Responses per unit time as a function of responses required per interval on conjoint schedule.
Herrnstein, R. J., and Morse, W. H. "A Conjunctive Schedule of Reinforcement." *Journal of the Experimental Analysis of Behavior, 1,* No. 1 (Jan., 1958), 15–24; Fig. 1, p. 17.

IV-16 Cumulative-record segments comparing performance on FI 15 TO 5 with that of conjoint FI 15 FR 40 TO 5 schedule.
Herrnstein, R. J., and Morse, W. H., "A Conjunctive Schedule of Reinforcement." *Journal of the Experimental Analysis of Behavior, 1,* No. 1 (Jan., 1958), 15–24; Fig. 4, p. 19.

IV-22 Contingencies of alternative FRFI and conjoint FRFI schedules.

IV-27 Stylized curve showing performance on an adjusting schedule.

IV-30 Cumulative record of performance on schedules with various minimum IRT requirements.
Kelleher, R. T., Fry, W., and Cook, L., "Adjusting Fixed-ratio Schedules in the Squirrel Monkey." *Journal of the Experimental Analysis of Behavior, 7,* No. 1 (Jan., 1964), 69–77; Fig. 1, p. 71.

IV-31 Mean FR values with minimal IRT requirements.
Kelleher, R. T., Fry, W., and Cook, L., "Adjusting Fixed-

Section V

MULTIOPERANT REPERTOIRES

HIGHER ORDER REINFORCEMENT SCHEDULES

Linear and Parallel Reinforcement-Schedule Arrangements Forming Higher Order Schedules

V-1

Although many of the behavioral samples discussed to this point have been temporally extended, and some substantial, the relation of such behavioral units to behavior of the order of complexity commonly seen outside the laboratory remains unclear. Recent research has provided suggestions for empirical steps bridging this chasm. /

V-2

These developments are based on two kinds of evidence. (1) Linear arrangements of behavior can be combined into larger units, not merely by chain, tandem, multiple, or mixed scheduling, but by treating behavior specified by a single scheduled contingency as an operant, reinforced on another schedule. (2) Parallel arrangements of operants and combinations of parallel arrangements generate more stable behavior, more extended patterns, and behavior which more closely approximates that found outside the laboratory. /

V-3

The recent developments in research that provide a

275

possible means for the analysis of complex behavior include (1) treating behavior specified by one scheduled contingency as a(n) _____, and reinforcing it on another schedule, thereby using (linear, parallel) arrangements of behavior; and (2) combinations of simultaneously ongoing and/or option situations, thereby using _____ arrangements of behavior. /

operant
linear
parallel

V-4

A behavior unit composed of a single specified schedule contingency (e.g., FI 4), which is in turn reinforced on another schedule contingency, is called a *higher order schedule*. For example, following completion of an FI 4, a light is briefly illuminated and 15 such FI 4 units, both light and food, are presented. This is called a(n) _____ schedule and would be symbolized FR 15 (FI 4). /

higher order

V-5

If the FI 4 unit operates as an operant, few or no FI 4 units should occur immediately following food presentation. This should be followed by a series of FI 4 units at a higher rate, terminating in food reinforcement. That is, there would be a(n) _____ after reinforcement, followed by a series of units at somewhat higher response rates. /

pause

V-6

The sample cumulative record shown illustrates such higher schedule control. Notice that each unit (FI 4) is generally like an FI, and the overall shape of the record is like a(n) _____. There are few _____ units exhibiting scalloping immediately following food reinforcement, but approaching terminal reinforcement progressively greater scalloping and higher rates, indicated by the arrow (pips indicate brief light flashes). /

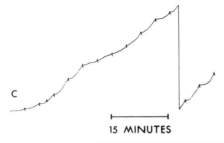

C

|—————————————|
15 MINUTES

FI
FI

V-7

The importance of such _____ order schedules is that they show that the basic schedule (FI 4 in the preceding example) can function as a reinforceable unit. /

higher

V-8

The basic unit operant can be considered the first order schedule (e.g., FI 4); the overall schedule [e.g., FR 15 (FI 4)] can be called a second _____ operant. /

order

V-9

Thus, in a schedule defined by the contingencies FR 5 (FR 20), the first order schedule would be FR _____, and the *second order schedule would be* _____●
_____ _____. /

20
FR 5 (FR 20)

V-10

In the preceding example, _____ suc-

277

cessive FR _____ units would be required for reinforcement. /

5
20

V-11

In addition to being a higher order schedule, since it has two levels of contingencies, this would be an example of a(n) _____ order schedule. /

second

V-12

It follows that a schedule in which three successive units of FI 4 are reinforced on an FR 15 schedule, that is, FR 3 [FR 15 (FI 4)], would be called a(n) _____●
_____ order schedule, since it has three levels of contingencies. /

third

V-13

However, all such multilevel schedules (i.e., second order, third order) fall within the general class of _____ order schedules. /

higher

V-14

Explicit research on higher order schedules has been relatively recent. However, a number of investigators have used higher order schedules for other experimental purposes without dealing with this implication of these schedules. /

V-15

For example, a two member FI chained schedule, where both members are of equal length, could also be expressed as a second order schedule. If the FIs were 1 minute, the appropriate notation would be FR 2 (FI 1). Similarly, a five member chained schedule composed of FI 2 units would be symbolized _____●
_____ _____. /

278

V-16

Four basic ways of studying second order chained schedules have been described: (1) tandem schedules, (2) chained schedules, (3) variable chains, and (4) schedules with brief stimulus changes. /

V-17

As with simple tandem schedules, there is (no, an) exteroceptive stimulus change correlated with component performances in second order tandem schedules. /

no

V-18

The figure shows sample cumulative records of Tand FR 3 (FI 1) performance. The overall performance resembles that seen in a simple _____.
Notice the overall _____ acceleration, with little scalloping in individual components. /

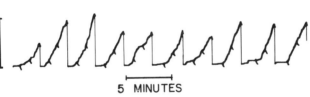

FI
positive

V-19

Thus, in second order tandem schedules individual units (e.g., FI 1) can be reinforced as operants but exhibit little _____. /

scalloping

V-20

In second order *chained* schedules, overall performances often reflect the second order schedule control, and performance in individual first order schedules often reflects appropriate schedule control as well. /

V-21

Consider chain FR 5 (FI 2) and simple FI 10. In both cases, food reinforcement is forthcoming _____ minutes after the last reinforced responses. /

10

V-22

In the cumulative records shown, performance prior to the first reinforcement was not included, since extensive pausing occurred in the first component of the second order chain. However, the response rate within subsequent components was generally _____ accelerated, and the overall rate terminating in food reinforcement was positively accelerated. (Session numbers are at the left of the segments.) /

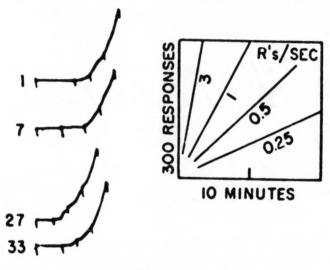

positively

V-23

FI 10, on the other hand, is very (well, poorly) main-

280

tained, if at all, and is often interrupted by very long pauses in the same subjects. /

poorly

V-24

The rather poor performances in early members of such chained second order schedules are clarified somewhat if a variable interval schedule is substituted for the fixed interval schedule as the first order operant. The sample cumulative records from chain FR 5 (VI 1) and chain FR 5 (FI 1) illustrate the great difference. (Dots over the segments indicate food reinforcement.) /

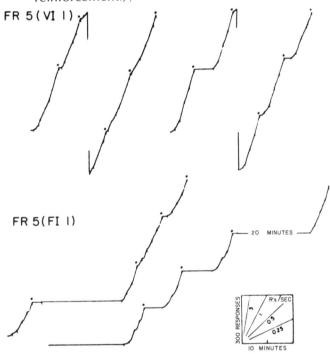

FR 5 (VI 1)

FR 5 (FI 1)

20 MINUTES

300 RESPONSES

R's /SEC

10 MINUTES

V-25

The extended pausing and occasional intermediate rates which are common in the _____ performance are generally absent from the _____● _____ record. /

FI
VI

The interpretation of this difference is not entirely clear. One suggestion has been that occasionally all five components in the VI schedule may be relatively short, thereby moving the first component much closer to the terminal food reinforcer than the first component of the FI schedule. This should (weaken, strengthen) the stimulus controlling properties of early stimuli in the VI schedule. /

strengthen

Much longer behavioral sequences have been maintained using variable interval schedules as the first order operant, although extended pausing emerges. The following sample records show FR 10 (VI 3) and FR 20 (VI 3) for a pigeon. At the higher ratio, note the extended _____, although the running rate was still relatively high. /

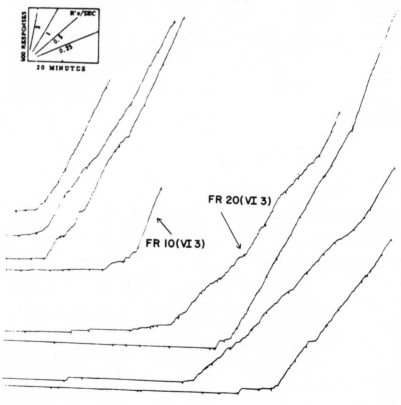

V-28

Second order chain FR (FR) schedules were discussed earlier when we dealt with added counters. For example, if every peck on a key increases the size of an illuminated slit on the key, and 70 pecks provides reinforcement and returns the slit to its beginning size, this would be a FR 70 (FR 1) schedule. /

V-29

This added counter procedure permits an assessment of the role of second order chain FR (FR 1) scheduling in maintaining performance. The figure shows FR 420 (A), with transition to FR 420 (FR 1) (B), followed by characteristic performance on the same second order schedule (C). /

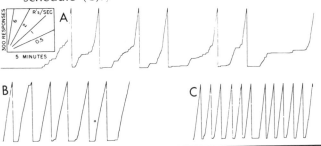

V-30

Nearly all local rate variability is eliminated by B, and post-reinforcement pausing is markedly (increased, reduced). /

reduced

V-31

The characteristic performance (C) shows _____●
_____ local rate and extremely short post-reinforcement pausing. /

no

V-32

If added counter schedules are changed such that

more than one response is required to change the slit size, the schedule becomes a *block added counter*. For example, if every 35 responses changed the slit size, and four changes in slit size were required per reinforcement, this would be symbolized chain ____●

_____. /

FR 4 (FR 35)

Thus, the second order schedule chain FR 10 (FR 5), in which every fifth response increased slit size and every tenth increase in slit size produced reinforcement, could also be called a ratio schedule with a(n)

_____ _____ _____. /

block added counter

Unlike the simple added counter, the block added counter produces longer post-reinforcement pauses. The cumulative record shows transition from FR 140 (A) to characteristic performance on FR 4 (FR 35) with block added counter. /

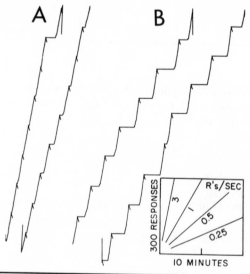

The length of post-reinforcement pauses are far

longer in *B* than in *A* causing an overall rate _____●
_____. /

decrease (or equivalent
answer)

Another chain FR (FR) schedule which has been
studied for some time without explicit reference to
higher order scheduling has been called a *token reinforcement schedule.* In such a schedule, tokens
(e.g., such objects as poker chips may be used) are
obtained on one schedule, then a second schedule
is used to exchange the tokens for an unconditioned
reinforcer. /

In such _____ schedules, two contingencies must be considered: (1) the schedule under
which the tokens are obtained, or the _____●
_____ order schedule; and (2) the
schedule under which the tokens may be used to
obtain the primary reinforcer. /

token
first

If every 125 responses gave the animal a token, and
50 tokens must be exchanged for food, this would
be symbolized as a(n) _____ schedule. /

FR 50 (FR 125)

The cumulative record shows a FR 50 (FR 125) second order token schedule. As with other very extended chained schedules, there is considerable ___●
_____ in the early components. /

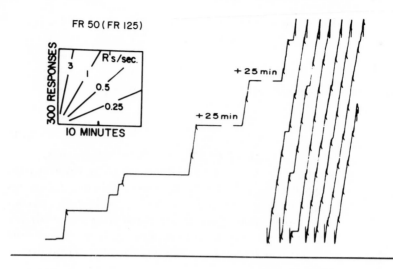

FR 50 (FR 125)

300 RESPONSES

3
1
R's/sec.
0.5
0.25

10 MINUTES

+ 25 min

+ 25 min

---

pausing

V-40

Early individual components (FR 125) reveal a post-reinforcement pause followed by a high running rate, as would be expected with a simple FR. In addition, the overall performance on the second order schedule FR 50 (FR 125) is also like a simple FR, with a post-reinforcement pause, shifting to a high _____●
_____ rate. /

running

V-41

Thus far we have discussed tandem and chained second order schedules. In tandem schedules it was found there were no appreciable differences between the tandem schedule and a(n) _____ schedule equal to the sum of the components of the tandem schedule. /

simple

V-42

In extended chained schedules, where the components are presented in a fixed sequence, substantial pausing typically appears in the (early, late) components of the chain./

286

V-43

Earlier in the program, in discussing chained schedules, it was suggested that the weakness of early
members of the chain was due to the ineffectiveness
of the discriminative stimuli in early components as
_____ _____./

conditioned reinforcers

V-44

Perhaps the differences in conditioned reinforcing
properties of stimuli associated with members of a
chain could be minimized by varying the order in
the sequence in which members of the chain and
their associated discriminative stimuli occur from one
chain to the next./

V-45

A sequence in which the order of the components is
changed is called a *variable chain*. If a chain is composed of three FI 1.5 components, the order of which
is randomized, this would be abbreviated *var chain*
_____./

FR 3 (FI 1.5)

V-46

Cumulative records comparing the effectiveness of
chain FR 3 (FI 1.5) (*A*) and var chain FR 3 (FI 1.5) (*B*)
in maintaining behavior are shown./

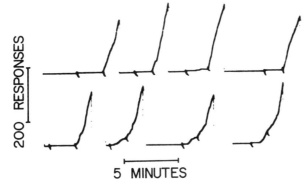

Prolonged _____ developed in the
chain condition, while the _____ ___•
_____ was more effective in maintain-
ing the characteristic performance of the individual
components. /

pausing
var chain

The primary advantage of the var chain schedule is
that each stimulus is established as an effective conditioned _____. The same goal can be
achieved by momentarily presenting the same conditioned reinforcing stimulus after completion of
each behavioral unit. /

reinforcer

A second order schedule in which such a *brief* presentation of the conditioned reinforcing stimulus is
used to maintain the first order components is called
a(n) _____ *stimulus second order*
schedule. /

brief

The lamp inside the reinforcement dispenser in a
conditioning chamber is often illuminated briefly
when food is delivered. Such a stimulus could be
presented briefly intermittently during a larger programmed contingency, as a potential _____
reinforcer. /

conditioned

For example, if every 400th response was initially followed by illumination of the food hopper, plus food
presentation, the food hopper light may become a

conditioned reinforcer. Subsequently, the light could be presented alone after the 400th, 800th, etc., response, with food coming at the end of a series of ratios of 400. The cumulative record shows performance established in this way in which 10 ratios of 400 were required for food reinforcement. This would be symbolized _____ (_____ : flash).

FR 10 (FR 400 : flash)

V-52

In the foregoing unconditioned reinforcement schedule, _____ responses were required per reinforcement. /

4000

V-53

Compare the performance of the same animal on the FR 10 (400 : flash) schedule shown in the preceding figure with a simple FR 4000 shown in this figure, keeping in mind that the same number of responses were required per food reinforcement. /

V-54

The effect of the brief stimulus on pausing is shown more clearly by these frequency distributions of pause

lengths during the red light (FR 4000) and green light
FR 10 (FR 400 : flash). /

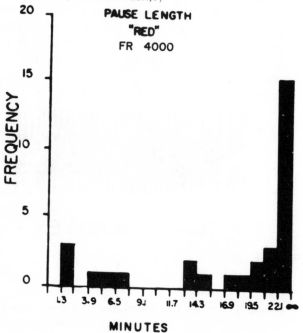

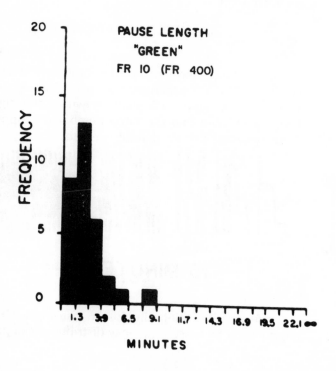

The pause length during the red light (i.e., FR 4000) was (very long, relatively short); the pause length before the FR 10 (FR 400 : flash) was (very long, relatively short). /

very long
relatively short

In another animal, the same basic procedure was used to establish a much more extended second order schedule in which performance was maintained on an FR 30 (FR 400 : flash) (i.e., 120,000 responses for food reinforcement) schedule. No extensive pausing developed (records not shown). /

Somewhat less dramatic, but equally significant second order schedule control has been demonstrated with FR (FR) and FR (FI) brief stimulus schedules. /

Pigeons reinforced on a FI 10 (FR 20 : white light) schedule produced performance revealing control of both contingencies, as shown in the figure (pips = light; pen reset = food presentation). /

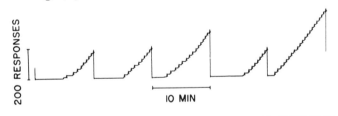

The first order schedule clearly shows "pause-and-run" performance characteristic of _____ _____ schedules, and the overall character of the sequence of FR 20s is gradually positively accelerated, as one would expect with simple _____● _____ _____ schedules. /

fixed ratio

fixed interval

V-60

In the foregoing case, behavior maintained by the
_____ _____ schedules
was serving as an operant, which was being reinforced on a(n) _____ _____
schedule. /

fixed ratio

fixed interval

V-61

Reversing the order of ratio and interval schedules in
second order schedules can lead to variable results,
depending on schedule parameters. The cumulative
record here shows performance for a pigeon on FR
30 (FI 2 : white light) (*A*) and FR 15 (FR 4 : white light)
(*B*). /

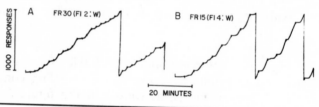

V-62

At FR 30 (FI 2 : W), individual first order components
are clearly like simple _____ _____●
_____ performance. /

fixed interval or *FI 2*

V-63

At FR 15 (FI 4: W), however, both first and second
order performances are schedule-appropriate, with
runs of FI 4s at a higher running rate. /

V-64

Data for another bird confirm the ratio control of the
second order schedule, as expressed in the figure. /

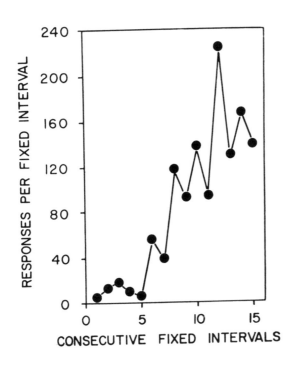

Notice the extremely _____ rates for
the first five FIs, followed by progressively increasing
rates for the remainder of the operant units. /

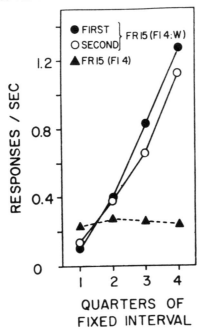

V-66

Control exercised by the first order schedule (FI in this case) can be seen by examining response rates during successive quarters of the fixed intervals. The graph shows the number of responses during each quarter of the FI components for FR 15 (FI 4 : W). /

V-67

The curves connecting circles indicate rates over successive quarters of all FIs. The rates increase progressively over the FIs, indicating that the characteristic performance of the first order schedule has (been, not been) retained. /

been

V-68

The lines connecting triangles along the bottom of the graph show the change in rate following discontinuation of brief stimulus which had previously been presented at the end of each FI. The rate across the FI without the brief stimulus (increases, remains constant, decreases), indicating that the brief stimulus is essential to maintain fixed interval schedule control over the first order schedule. /

remains constant

V-69

An interesting problem is posed by second order FR (IRT > t) schedules. It will be recalled that *IRT > t* schedules require responses to be spaced certain intervals apart to be reinforced. That is, they tend to generate (low, high) rates. FR schedules, on the other hand, tend to generate (low, high) rates. /

low
high

V-70

The combination of the two kinds of contingencies

poses a predictive dilemma. In an FR 3 (IRT > 8 sec: flash) schedule, would one expect the overall rate to be high or low? Presumably the rate during first-order components should be _____, while the overall feature of the schedule should be a _____ rate. /

low
high

V-71

The figure shows response rates during the first, second, and third components of *brief stimulus* FR 3 (IRT > 8 sec), Tand FR 3 (IRT > 8 sec), and Chain FR 3 (IRT > 8 sec) schedules. /

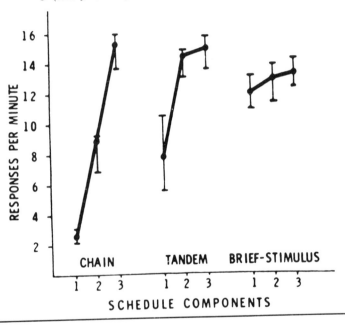

V-72

The rates during the third component were (highest, lowest) in the brief stimulus schedule, but were (highest, lowest) during the first component for the brief stimulus schedule. /

lowest
highest

The net effect is that the overall rate is higher in brief stimulus schedules, but that the brief stimulus schedule has a higher frequency of reinforcement because the rate during the third component (which leads to primary reinforcement) is _____. /

lowest

Thus, the brief stimulus schedule tends to keep overall rate more constant, and relatively _____. This is presumably due to the greater _____ reinforcing properties of the brief stimulus. /

high
conditioned

In introducing higher order schedules, we referred to the possibility that a second order schedule could be reinforced on yet another schedule. Such a complex contingency is called a third order reinforcement schedule. /

Consider a second order schedule in which every 40 responses is followed by a flash of the feeder light, and three FR 40: flash completions leads to food. This would be written _____. /

FR 3 (FR 40 : flash)

If an additional contingency that three such second-order schedules must be completed per food reinforcement is instated, this becomes a(n) _____●
_____ order schedule, designated FR 3 [FR 3 (FR 40)]. /

third

To maintain the characteristic performance of the

second order schedule as a unit, a second conditioned reinforcer must be presented following each
completion of FR 3 (FR 40 : flash). For example, if
both a tone and light were presented during food
reinforcement, the light could be presented following each FR 40 and the tone could be presented following each FR 3 (FR 40 : flash). /

V-79

For notational convenience, the stimulus presented
following each first order component will be designated S_1 and the stimulus presented after each second component, S_2. In the preceding example, S_1
would be _____ and S_2 _____●
_____ . /

light
tone

V-80

The following cumulative record illustrates FR 3 [FR
3 (FR 40 : S_1) : S_2] by a rat. Notice the _____

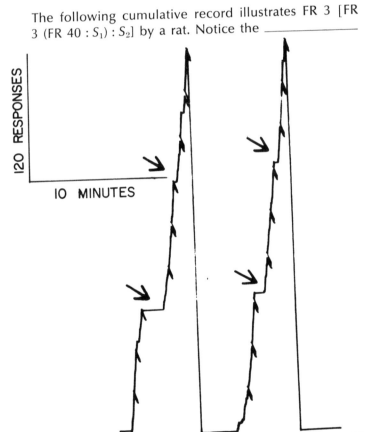

pauses after the terminal component, and the ratio-like quality of each individual first order component (pips $= S_1$; arrows $= S_2$; pen reset $=$ food). /

long

V-81

The control exerted by the third order schedule can be illustrated by examining the length of time required to complete each ratio (i.e., a pause measure). In a FR 3 [FR 3 (FR 40 : S_1) : S_2] schedule, there are nine ratios, each with a pause. The figure shows median time in ratios 2 through 9 on this schedule. /

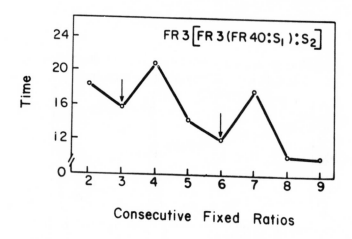

Consecutive Fixed Ratios

V-82

Pauses occur in ratios 4 and _____, which correspond to the post-reinforcement pauses following completion of each second order component. /

7

V-83

Removal of the second order stimuli eliminates second order post-reinforcement pausing, as can be seen in the figure, comparing time to complete successive fixed ratios of a second-order schedule requiring the same total number of responses, FR 9 (FR 40 : S_1). /

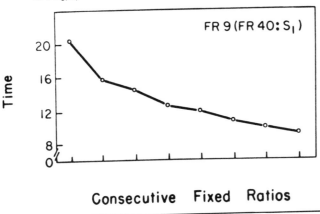

Consecutive Fixed Ratios

In other words, the brief stimulus contingent on completing the second order schedule FR 3 (FR 40 : S_1) was reinforcing the entire second order schedule as a unit. The second order schedule was acting as a(n) _____ . /

operant

As can be seen from these data, the post-reinforcement pause following the second order schedule emerges in both cases, despite the difference in numbers of required ratios and the ratio sizes. /

Thus, it is apparent that second order schedules can be differentially reinforced as _____ and are subject to manipulations of schedule parameters much as simple operants can be manipulated. /

operants

Combinations of Serial and Parallel Operants and Higher-Order Schedules of Multioperants

Research on higher-order scheduling has shown that larger and more complex units of behavior can function as _____. /

operants

The higher-order schedules discussed to this point have been very limited. That is, we have dealt with FI, FR, and DRL schedules in combinations. Although studies are admittedly conceptually important, the behavior generated by such schedules is still impoverished relative to the very heterogeneous behavior seen outside the laboratory. /

The rudiments of more complex behavior can be seen if we shift our attention to parallel arrangements of operants and combinations of serial and parallel arrangements. In an earlier section it may be recalled that a parallel arrangement of two operants is called a(n) _____. /

option

The following lists the components of a nonreversible option maintained by food and water reinforcement:

1. VR 100   red light   food reinforcement
2. FR 100   gren light   water reinforcement

In this situation initiation of responding in one component precludes responding in the other until completion of the component's requirements. /

If we change the foregoing schedule such that a simple ratio contingency must be satisfied before the option contingencies become available, we have the basic unit of more complex scheduling, called a tree. /

If an FR 5 contingency must be satisfied before the two S^D lights for VR 100 and FR 100 are illuminated, the entire schedule would be called a(n) _____●
_____, since it is composed of a single operant leading to an option. /

tree

That is, the opportunity to engage in either component of the operant is preceded by an FR requirement. Therefore, the FR requirement must be completed _____ to engaging in VR 100 or FR 100. /

prior

In an experiment a tree composed of an FR 80 leading to a nonreversible option the components of which are an FR 80 reinforced by water and an FR 80 reinforced by food was used. /

Following the initial FR 80 the subject (a baboon) has available a (reversible, nonreversible) option. /

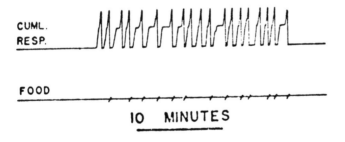

nonreversible

The cumulative records shown illustrate the overall performance (on the left) and detailed cumulative records of behavior maintained by these contingencies. In the records on the right, the pen resets

301

each time a food or water reinforcement is received, and _____ reinforcements are marked on the baseline events' pen. /

food

V-97

Notice that there was a characteristic run of responses during the first member of the tree, followed by another approximately equally sized number of responses. /

V-98

A tree such as the foregoing provides for a "choice" between schedules for attaining a given reinforcer or two reinforcers. Another method for assessing "preference" between schedules has been described earlier as a *switching procedure*. Its general feature consists of a sequence of options in which one part of each option provides for the attainment of un-conditioned reinforcement and the other part allows advancement to the next option. /

V-99

The following describes a switching procedure in which a pigeon was reinforced with grain for pecking an illuminated key. The color of the key was either red or green: A fixed-ratio schedule was associated with red and an IRT > t schedule with green. Once presented, a given color and its associated schedule remained in effect for a minimum of one reinforce-ment but could remain in effect up to a given maxi-mum number of reinforcements. After the first rein-forcement in a given color (red or green), a second key was illuminated white. At the t point the bird had the option of continuing on the previous schedule or completing a ratio on the white key. Completing a ratio on the white key changed the color of the key on the food-reinforcement schedule to the alter-native color and its associated schedule. Thus, by pecking the white key, the bird could control the schedule of food reinforcement. This sequence in-volves a switching procedure. That is, by emitting re-

sponses on the white key the bird could _____
_____ from one schedule to the other. /

switch

The FR requirement on the white key is called the *FR-to-switch*. Differences in pattern of responding on this key should reflect relative reinforcing properties of the red (FR, IRT) (schedule) and green (FR, IRT) (schedule) conditions. /

FR
IRT

In addition to the kinds and values of the two schedules, other factors can markedly influence switching. The maximum number of reinforcements under the two schedule conditions and the size of the FR-to-_____ can also be important. /

switch

Consider the cumulative records shown, where the IRT > t schedule was held at 10 seconds, and the size of FR for food reinforcement varied from 25 to 400. The event pen is up during the IRT > t period and down during _____ periods. The small cumulative record on the right is the FR-switching performance. /

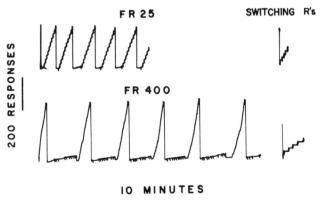

V-103

Notice that at FR 25 the lengths of the IRT $>$ t periods are much shorter than in the FR 400 schedule condition. In addition, the switching rate is _____ under the FR 25 conditions (i.e., the animal was switching to the FR 25 condition with higher frequency). /

higher

V-104

Thus, the relative values of the schedules can be important determinants of time spent in each schedule condition and the rate of _____. /

switching

V-105

When the maximum number of reinforcements in a given schedule is manipulated, we also see a change in time spent during each component and frequency of switching. In the following cumulative records IRT $>$ 10 sec FR 200 schedules were in effect in both cases. The upper records show performance when the maximum number of reinforcements in the IRT $>$ 10 sec schedule was set at 20, and the lower records where the maximum was set at 2 reinforcements. /

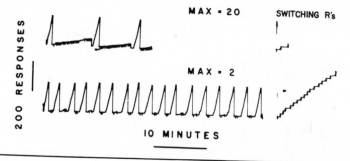

V-106

The amount of time spent in the IRT $>$ 10 sec condition was relatively (short, long) at the 20 reinforcement maximum, and the rate of switching was relatively (high, low) at the 2 reinforcement maximum. (Compare time/component and number of switching responses.) /

long
high

V-107

In the preceding examples, the FR-to-switch schedule value has been maintained at 10. When the number of responses to switch is manipulated, it not only changes switching performance but the time in each schedule condition. The upper record shows IRT > 10, and FR 200 with the ratio to switch at FR 10 as before. The lower records are at a ratio to switch of FR 80. The switching performance is clearly different. In addition, it appears the subject tended to remain in the less preferred schedule longer under the high ratio-to-switch condition. /

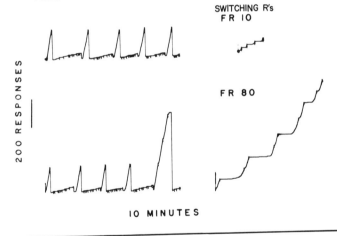

V-108

Emerging from these studies with trees and switching is the impression that parallel arrangements and combinations of parallel arrangements create more complex behavior than can be generated using serial reinforcement contingencies. The extent to which such more complex parallel arrangements retain uni-

305

tary properties (i.e., are capable of acting as a reinforceable response unit) has not been discussed. /

In an experiment, a tree was established composed
of FR 20 components in which the initial FR 20 provided access to a nonreversible option one component of which was an FR 20 reinforced by water
and the other an FR 20 reinforced by food. Once
performance on this schedule (tree) had stabilized,
the entire behavioral unit (i.e., the tree) was reinforced on a IRT > 2 schedule. /

The cumulative records shown illustrate basic performance on this second-order schedule, IRT>2
[FR 20 $\frac{(FR\ 20)}{(FR\ 20)}$]. This lower record is a detail of successive ratio runs indicating spacing of ratios con-
trolled by the IRT contingency. The ratios are spaced
very regularly at 2-minute intervals. Thus, the tree was
acting as a(n) _____ which could be
reinforced on another schedule (an IRT>2-minute
schedule in this case). /

CUMUL. RESP.

20 MINUTES

---

operant or *unit*

A similar second-order schedule was generated by
developing a tree composed of FR 40 components.
In this case the entire tree was reinforced on an FR 4
schedule. /

The cumulative records here show characteristic pause and run performance. The pen resets after every 80 responses, and marks a pip at food reinforcement. Notice the long _____ pauses between successive ratio runs, then groups of 4 FR 80s. Once again, the tree was acting as a reinforceable unit, in this case reinforced on a(n) ____● _____ schedule. /

CUMUL. RESP. —————

20 MINUTES

post-reinforcement
FR 4

Perhaps the most complex and convincing demonstration of the unitary properties of a tree as a reinforceable unit has been by placing a tree composed of FR 20 units on a multiple second-order schedule: under one stimulus condition on a IRT > 2-minute schedule, and under other stimulus conditions on an FR 4 schedule. That is, functionally the tree, as a unit, was an operant under stimulus control, and the rate of its occurrence was determined by alternating stimulus conditions. /

CUMUL. RESP.

20 MINUTES

The cumulative record here shows spacing of responses appropriate to the FR and IRT contingencies under appropriate stimulus conditions. The tree is clearly a powerful and viable response unit. /

307

Multioperant Analysis of Social Behavior and Continuous Behavioral Repertoires

V-115

The behavioral cases discussed thus far have involved individual organisms and relatively limited behavioral samples. The foregoing analysis lends itself equally to investigating interactions between organisms and to the study of continuous and highly complex behavior sequences. /

V-116

A relatively simple multiorganism example involves mutual reinforcement by two animals. For example, two monkeys placed in adjacent chambers were conditioned to present food to one another. In the presence of a white light, monkey A presses a lever on a fixed-ratio schedule. The consequences of completing this contingency are that a red light is presented to monkey A, and monkey B receives food and a white light. In the presence of the white light, monkey B presses a lever on a FR schedule feeding monkey A. /

V-117

Thus, the two animals alternate in working to feed one another; both work on a FR schedule in the presence of a(n) _____ light, which produces a(n) _____ light for the working animal and food for the paired animal. /

white

red

V-118

The figure shows sample cumulative records of FR 32 performance in the alternating feeding procedure. Notice the relatively high and stable rates, with occasional irregularities in the form of knees and intermediate rates. /

308

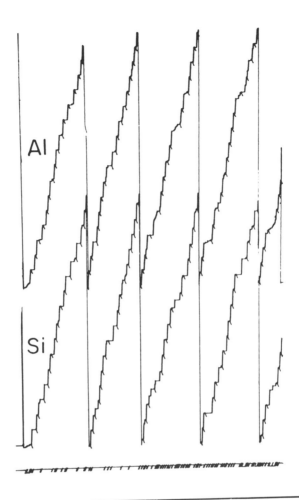

Al

Si

To what extent is the FR performance maintained by the stimuli associated with feeding the second animal as opposed to the delayed food presentation by the paired animal? Contingencies were changed such that alternation was not required (i.e., both monkeys could feed each other in any order at any time). If feeding the paired animal was a powerful reinforcer, one would expect the FR performance to be (weakened, maintained) under nonalternation contingencies. /

maintained

If the behavior was primarily controlled by the paired animal's feeding a given monkey following his FR performance, the performance might be expected to be (weakened, maintained) under the nonalternation contingencies. The figure shows the number of responses per minute over 30 consecutive sessions on these contingencies. /

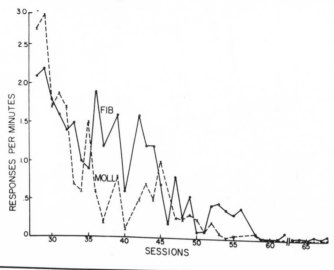

weakened

The rapid decline in response rate, with an ultimate cessation of responding, indicates that presenting food to the paired animal (was, was not) maintaining the FR performance. /

was not

The figure reveals the deterioration of the mutual feeding behavior under the nonalternation contingencies from the second and twenty-fourth sessions. /

310

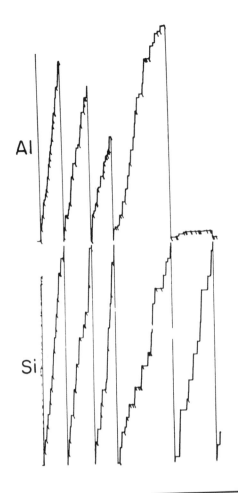

Notice that monkey _____ continued
feeding monkey _____ far longer than
the reverse. Indeed, by the twenty-fourth session,
monkey _____ had ceased responding
altogether, but was still being fed occasionally by
monkey _____. /

A
B
B
A

In another more complex situation two monkeys obtain food, water, fruit, and morphine injections as reinforcing consequences. Every two hours a light is illuminated on an electronically locked door, indicating to monkey A that if he stands on a platform scale, the door will unlock, providing access to the work chamber. When he enters the work chamber and closes the door, an S^D light is presented, indicating to monkey B that if he stands on a platform outside an adjacent chamber, the electronically locked door will unlock and give him access to that compartment. /

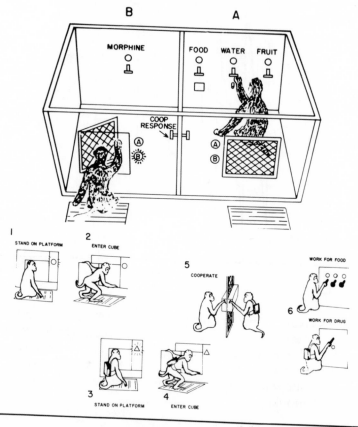

Once both animals are inside their respective compartments, two "cooperative" switches on the transparent wall that separates the two compartments are operable. If both animals hold their switches down simultaneously for 10 seconds, S^D lights on their respective work panels will be illuminated. For monkey A, lights indicating ⏤⏤⏤⏤⏤⏤, ⏤⏤⏤⏤⏤● ⏤⏤⏤⏤⏤⏤⏤, and ⏤⏤⏤⏤⏤⏤ can be obtained, and for monkey B and S^D light indicating ⏤⏤⏤⏤⏤⏤ can be obtained intravenously. /

food, water, (and) fruit
morphine

After working for their respective reinforcers the two animals can leave their work compartments and obtain ⏤⏤⏤⏤⏤⏤⏤ in a common third compartment. /

juice

As can be seen, an alternation procedure is used to establish access to the respective work chambers. That is, monkey A turns on the S^D for monkey ⏤⏤● ⏤⏤⏤⏤⏤⏤⏤, and monkey B's entrance makes available the ⏤⏤⏤⏤⏤⏤ response switches. /

B
cooperative

When the two cooperative switches have been closed for 10 seconds, monkey A has available a three-member nonreversible option while monkey B has a simple FR schedule. /

When the program recycles, the S^D for monkey B to enter the food, water, and fruit chamber is presented first, and following monkey B's entrance the S^D for monkey ⏤⏤⏤⏤⏤⏤ to enter the morphine compartment is presented. /

A

Thus, each animal has the opportunity to present the S^D for food, water, and fruit and for morphine self-injection to the other animal, and each animal emits the cooperative response, sometimes giving access to food, water, and fruit and at other times giving access to _____. /

morphine

The figure shows sample cumulative records of performance by the two monkeys during a single behavioral cycle. The various points in the series of interactions and the behavior series are marked along the top of the figure. /

The foregoing multioperant program involves relatively complex social interdependencies in which the behavior of each animal provides the necessary condition for the behavior of the paired animal to be reinforced. In addition, each total behavior sequence lasts from 15 minutes to 1 hour, with the program recycling every 2 hours. Thus, from 12.5 to 50 percent of the animal's time is spent in programmed activities. /

Using similar, although much more complex contingencies, it has been found that 93 to 94 percent of a human subject's time could be brought under the control of scheduled contingencies in a controlled experimental environment. In this case an adult human subject lived in a three-room experimental apartment for 5 months, shown in the figure. /

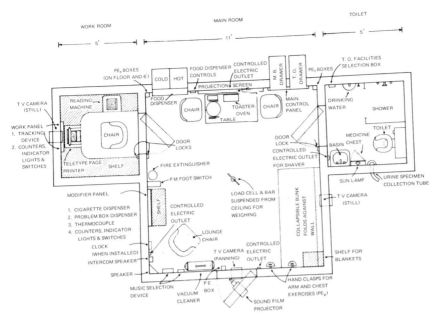

Diagram of experimental chamber showing furnishings and facilities in each room.

MAIN CONTROL PANEL

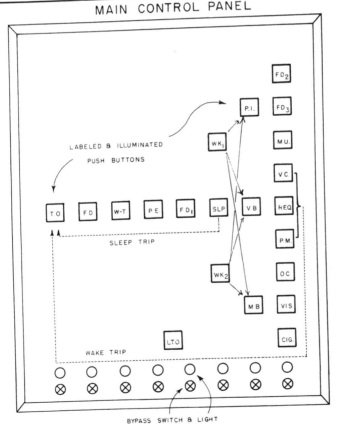

Provision was made for various activities, such as eating, reading, writing, oil painting, listening to music, oral communication, self-weighing and temperature measurement, and use of toilet facilities. The activities and contingencies were indicated to the subject on an illuminated pushbutton panel. /

In the following frames, refer to the figure at the foot of page 315 and the associated table. The beginning of each programmed cycle began with access to full toilet facilities, including a change of clothes (TO). Following completion of these activities the subject could indicate by pressing one of two buttons whether he would like to shorten the duration of the experiment or lengthen it (FD). /

Thus, TO and FD comprise a two-member _____●
_____. /

chain

On completing this chain the subject was provided with the opportunity to weigh himself using an electronic scale and to take his temperature with an electronic temperature recording thermometer, abbreviated _____ on the program. /

W-T

Following this, physical exercise was programmed, requiring the location of light randomly situated at various points in the experimental chamber, and lifting weights a fixed number of times (PE). This led to the opportunity to have a light snack from the food vendor, which provided a choice of several foods (FD 1). /

The program to this point has consisted of purely (parallel, serial) operants. /

serial

Following FD 1 a four member nonreversible option was programmed. Three of the members led to one set of consequences, the fourth led to a different kind of consequence. Pressing a button marked "sleep" would lower a bunk from the wall, lower the room temperature a few degrees, and extinguish the room lights. The subject could sleep as long as he wished, but on arising the program would recycle from _____●
_____. /

TO

The other three members of the option involved engaging in programmed instruction (PI); verbal behavior (VB), which meant typing on a teletypewriter; or manual behavior (MB), which included access to hobby materials. On completing one of these three activities, an eight-member _____ option became available. These responses and consequences are (1) major meal (three selections), (2) dessert, (3) music, (4) delayed variable consequence, (5) delayed access to forms for submitting written requests, (6) power maintenance, (7) earn delayed conversation via intercom, and (8) cigarettes. /

reversible

These contingencies were in effect for 152 days. The figure shows the distribution of time (in percent) the subject spent in some of the activities and groups of activities over the course of the experiment. /

317

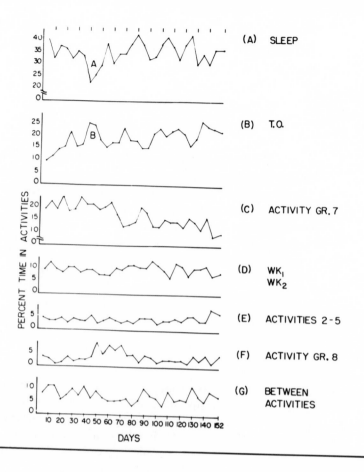

Y-axis label: PERCENT TIME IN ACTIVITIES
X-axis label: DAYS

(A) SLEEP
(B) T.O.
(C) ACTIVITY GR.7
(D) WK₁ WK₂
(E) ACTIVITIES 2-5
(F) ACTIVITY GR.8
(G) BETWEEN ACTIVITIES

V-143

While the percent time was relatively constant for most activities, the time in TO (decreased, increased) progressively, and the time in activity group 7 (decreased, increased) progressively over the 152 days. /

increased

decreased

V-144

Three of the more important operant classes responsible for maintaining the first five members in the multioperant program were programmed instruction, verbal behavior, and manual behavior (activity group 7). The opportunity to engage in these activities directly maintained behaviors preceding them. The

318

figure shows the cumulative time spent in these three activities over the 152 days of the experiment. /

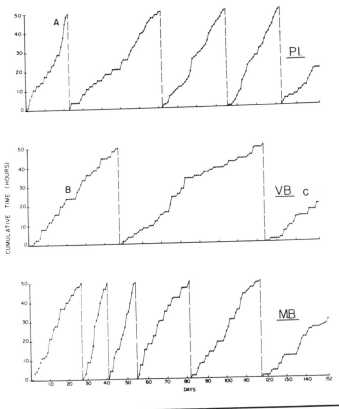

Notice the high rate of engaging in MB from days 30 through 50. During this period the subject was learning to oil-paint and spent considerable time in this activity. It is noteworthy that over the course of the experiment rates of all three activities (decreased, increased), suggesting that whatever consequences were programmed for these activities were not sufficient to maintain these behaviors at high levels. /

decreased

The availability of cigarettes in the terminal eight-member reversible option was usually maintained at a FR 25 contingency on a heavy button. During one subexperiment, the response requirement was systematically varied from FR 25 to FR 500, and the frequency of selecting cigarettes among the eight members of the option studied per opportunity. /

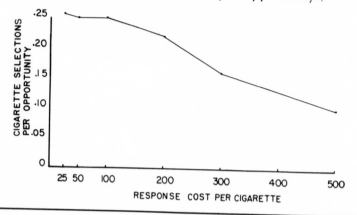

As can be seen, frequency of selecting this member of the option was (directly, inversely) related to ratio size. /

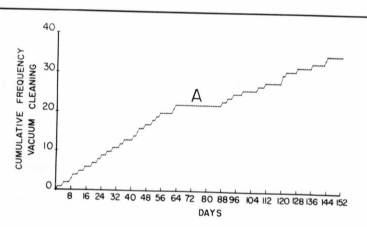

inversely

One of the activities available during TO was the opportunity to use a vacuum cleaner to clean the apartment. The figure shows the cumulative frequency of

320

use of the vacuum cleaner, which was very stable for the first 2 months. At A the rate (increased, decreased), then resumed at a low and more intermittent rate. The period marked A corresponds to the time when the FR requirement for cigarettes was placed at FR 500. /

decreased

V-149

Further support for the notion that the terminal consequences were not sufficiently effective in maintaining the behavioral repertoire is indicated in the following cumulative record of LTO (limited access to the toilet). During these periods, the subject failed to engage in any of the programmed activities. For all practical purposes, these intervals consisted of pauses of response-produced time outs. /

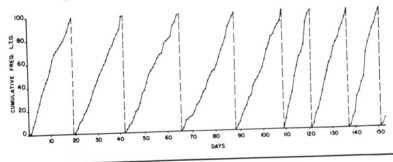

V-150

Over the course of the experiment, the frequency of LTO selection (decreased, increased) progressively. /

increased

V-151

Despite the decline in performance over the 5 months of social restriction, it was possible to maintain control over a large proportion of the subject's behavior. /

V-152

Among the more interesting findings of this experiment are (1) that large and apparently "normal" be-

321

havioral sequences are reinforcable as units; (2) it is possible to differentially manipulate portions of the total behavioral repertoire by changing reinforcement contingencies; (3) combinations of parallel and serial arrangements of operants are a powerful procedure for synthesizing complex multioperants; and (4) while many of the "usual" consequences are sufficient to maintain a great deal of highly complex behavior, progressive behavioral strain, as indicated by pausing, suggests that other arrangements of contingencies and/or other reinforcers may be necessary to more effectively maintain such behavior. /

Objectives

1 What is a higher order schedule?
V-2 to V-5

2 What two ways combining units of behavior may be made to obtain higher order schedules?
V-2, V-107

3 In a schedule FR 15 (FI 5), which schedule is the first-order schedule and which schedule is the second order schedule? Also, which operant is the first order operant and which operant is the second order operant?
V-4 to V-8

4 Give an example of a third order schedule in which each schedule is different.
V-12

5 What is the difference in performance between a chain FR 5 (FI2) and a FI 10?
V-21 to V-23 (chains, see III-3 to III-6)

6 What is the difference in contingencies between FR 100 and FR 100 (FR 1)?
V-28

7 An added counter provides a higher order sequence; what is the effect on behavior?
V-28 to V-31

8 What is a token reinforcement schedule?
V-26 to V-37

9 What two contingencies must be considered under token reinforcement schedules?
V-37

10 A token schedule is similar to which of the following sched-

ules: tandem schedule, chain schedule, multiple schedule, complex schedule?
V-39 to V-43

11 What is a variable chain schedule?
V-44 and V-45

12 What is the advantage of a variable chain schedule?
V-48

13 What is a brief stimulus schedule?
V-49

14 Which of the following three schedules tend to keep the overall rate more constant: brief stimulus, tandem, or chain?
V-73 and V-74

15 What is the best measure to use to examine the control that is exerted by a third order schedule?
V-81 to V-84

16 What is a tree?
V-90 to V-92

17 What are two ways of assessing schedule "preference?"
V-98

18 What is meant by "FR-to-switch," and what are the behavioral effects of altering the contingency?
V-100 and V-101, V-106 and V-107

19 If completion of the contingencies of one schedule is followed by an option (i.e., this sequence is a tree) and the entire behavioral unit is then reinforced on a schedule, what is the effect on behavior?
V-113 and V-114

20 The performance deteriorated in an experiment described in which monkeys engaged in cooperative feeding behavior. Why?
V-121 to V-123

21 Does the experiment involving cooperative morphine administration suggest that maintenance of multioperant repertoires is possible?
V-124 to V-132

22 What general categories of behavior were included in the multioperant situation using a human subject? Did they appear to be ordered in a fashion that provided reinforcement of less probable behaviors with the opportunity to engage in more probable behaviors?
V-134 to V-141

23 Whereas the percent time for most activities was relatively constant, the time of certain behaviors changed over the course of the experiment. Which behaviors changed and

what was the direction of change?
V-143 and V-144

24 Describe the course of percent time spent in programmed instruction, verbal behavior (teletype), and manual behaviors during the experiment with a human object.
V-144 and V-145

25 Describe the effect of increasing the fixed ratio size when cigarettes were the reinforcer.
V-146 and V-147

26 What was the relationship between increased fixed ratio size for cigarettes and vacuum cleaner use? Does this suggest a general behavioral disruption generated by the cigarette ratio contingency?
V-148

27 What supports the notion that the general situation became less reinforcing as the experiment progressed?
V-143 to V-145, V-149 to V-151

References

V-6 Cumulative records of performance on higher-order schedule showing extent of schedule control.
Kelleher, R. T., "Chaining and Conditioned Reinforcement" in *Operant Behavior: Areas of Research and Application*, W. K. Honig, ed. New York: Appleton-Century-Crofts, 1966; Fig. 11, p. 203.

V-18 Cumulative record of performance on a tandem FR 3 (FI 1) schedule.
Kelleher, R. T., and Fry, W. T., "Stimulus Functions in Chained Fixed-interval Schedules." *Journal of the Experimental Analysis of Behavior, 5*, No. 2 (April, 1962), 167–174; Fig. 3, p. 169.

V-22 Cumulative-record segments of performance on a second-order schedule.
Kelleher, R. T., and Gollub, L. R., "A Review of Positive Conditioned Reinforcement." *Journal of the Experimental Analysis of Behavior, 5*, No. 4 (Oct., 1962), 543; Fig. 9, p. 567.

V-24 Cumulative-record segments of performance on higher-order chain schedules.
Kelleher, R. T., and Gollub, L. R., "A Review of Positive Conditioned Reinforcement." *Journal of the Experimental Analysis of Behavior, 5*, No. 4 (Oct., 1962), 543; Fig. 12, p. 570.

V-58 Cumulative records showing schedule control with FI 10 (FR 20) brief stimulus schedule.

Findley, J. D., and Brady, J. V., "Facilitation of Large Ratio Performance by Use of Conditioned Reinforcement." *Journal of the Experimental Analysis of Behavior, 8*, No. 1 (Jan., 1965), 125–130; Fig. 1.

V-61 Cumulative records showing effect on performance of reversing order of ratio and interval components of second-order schedule.

Kelleher, R. T., "Conditioned Reinforcement in Second-order Schedules." *Journal of the Experimental Analysis of Behavior, 9*, No. 5 (Sept., 1966), 475–486; Fig. 1, p. 478.

V-64 Extent of ratio control in second-order schedule.

Kelleher, R. T., "Conditioned Reinforcement in Second-order Schedules." *Journal of the Experimental Analysis of Behavior, 9*, No. 5 (Sept., 1966), 475–486; Fig. 3, p. 479.

V-66 Rates during successive quarters of FI components of FR 15 (FI 4) schedule.

Kelleher, R. T., "Conditioned Reinforcement in Second-order Schedules." *Journal of the Experimental Analysis of Behavior, 9*, No. 5 (Sept., 1966), 475–486; Fig. 5, p. 480.

V-71 Performance resulting from FR 3 (IRT > 8 sec) as brief stimulus, tandem, and chain schedule.

Thomas, J. R., "Discriminative Time-out-avoidance in Pigeons." *Journal of the Experimental Analysis of Behavior, 8*, No. 5 (Sept., 1965), 329–338.

V-80 Cumulative records of third-order schedule performance.

Bigelow, G., and Thompson, T., "Third-order Fixed-ratio Schedules of Reinforcement." *Psychonomic Science, 13* (1968), 13–14.

V-81 Median time in ratios under third-order schedule.

Bigelow, G., and Thompson, T., "Third-order Fixed-ratio Schedules of Reinforcement." *Psychonomic Science, 13* (1968), 13–14.

V-83 Median time in ratios where schedule changed from FR 3 [FR 3 (FR 40 : S_1) S_2] to FR 9 (FR 40 : S_1).

Bigelow, G., and Thompson, T., "Third-order Fixed-ratio Schedules of Reinforcement." *Psychonomic Science, 13* (1968), 13–14.

V-102 Cumulative record of performance on IRT schedule combined with ratio requirements.

Findley, J. D., "An Experimental Outline for Building and Exploring Multi-operant Behavior Repertoires." *Journal of the Experimental Analysis of Behavior*, 5, No. 1, Supplement (Jan., 1962), Fig. 30, p. 149.

V-105 Cumulative record of performance on IRT > 10 sec FR 200 schedule with changes in maximum number of reinforcements.

Findley, J. D., "An Experimental Outline for Building and Exploring Multi-operant Behavior Repertoires." *Journal of the Experimental Analysis of Behavior*, 5, No. 1, Supplement (Jan., 1962), Fig. 31, p. 150.

V-107 Effect of changing FR to switch contingency on schedule with nonreversible option.

Findley, J. D., "An Experimental Outline for Building and Exploring Multi-operant Behavior Repertoires." *Journal of the Experimental Analysis of Behavior*, 5, No. 1, Supplement (Jan., 1962), Fig. 32, p. 151.

V-110 Cumulative record of performance on higher-order schedule in which tree is reinforced as an operant.

Findley, J. D., "An Experimental Outline for Building and Exploring Multi-operant Behavior Repertoires." *Journal of the Experimental Analysis of Behavior*, 5, No. 1, Supplement (Jan., 1962), Fig. 41, p. 158.

V-112 Cumulative record of characteristic performance generated by schedule in which tree is reinforced as an operant.

Findley, J. D., "An Experimental Outline for Building and Exploring Multi-operant Behavior Repertoires." *Journal of the Experimental Analysis of Behavior*, 5, No. 1, Supplement (Jan., 1962), Fig. 41, p. 158.

V-114 Cumulative record of performance generated by schedule in which tree is reinforced as an operant.

Findley, J. D., "An Experimental Outline for Building and Exploring Multi-operant Behavior Repertoires." *Journal of the Experimental Analysis of Behavior*, 5, No. 1, Supplement (Jan., 1962), Fig. 43, p. 160

V-118 Cumulative record of performance on FR 32 with animals cooperating and alternating in feeding.

Boren, J. J., "An Experimental Social Relation between Two Monkeys." *Journal of the Experimental Analysis of Behavior*, 9, No. 6 (Nov., 1966), 691–700.

V-120 Number of responses per minute over thirty consecutive sessions of the cooperating animals.

Boren, J. J., "An Experimental Social Relation between

Two Monkeys." *Journal of the Experimental Analysis of Behavior,* 9, No. 6 (Nov., 1966), 691–700; Fig. 3, p. 695.

V-122 Cumulative records illustrating deterioration of mutual feeding behavior performance.

Boren, J. J., "An Experimental Social Relation between Two Monkeys." *Journal of the Experimental Analysis of Behavior,* 9, No. 6 (Nov., 1966), 691–700; Fig. 7, p. 698.

V-124 Appearance of drug-social interaction chamber.

Thompson, T., Bigelow, G., and Pickens, R., "Environmental Variables Influencing Drug Self-administration" in *Stimulus Properties of Drugs,* T. Thompson and R. Pickens, eds. New York: Appleton-Century-Crofts, 1971.

V-131 Cumulative-record segments of performance by two animals in the drug-social chamber, monkeys.

Thompson, T., Bigelow, G., and Pickens, R., "Environmental Variables Influencing Drug Self-administration" in *Stimulus Properties of Drugs,* T. Thompson and R. Pickens, eds. New York: Appleton-Century-Crofts, 1971.

V-133 Experimental chamber showing human beings and facilities in each room.

Findley, J., "Programmed Environments for the Experimental Analysis of Human Behavior" in *Operant Behavior: Areas of Research and Application,* W. K. Honig, ed. New York: Appleton-Century-Crofts, 1966; Fig. 2, p. 835.

V-134 Main control panel containing pushbuttons that could be illuminated with each button labeled.

Findley, J., "Programmed Environments for the Experimental Analysis of Human Behavior" in *Operant Behavior: Areas of Research and Application,* W. K. Honig, ed. New York: Appleton-Century-Crofts, 1966; Fig. 1, p. 833.

V-142 Distribution of percent times the subject spent in some of the activities over the 152-day period, human being.

Findley, J., "Programmed Environments for the Experimental Analysis of Human Behavior" in *Operant Behavior: Areas of Research and Application,* W. K. Honig, ed. New York: Appleton-Century-Crofts, 1966; Fig. 3, p. 836.

V-144 Cumulative time spent in programmed instruction, verbal behavior (teletype), and manual behaviors (hobbies) for each day of the experiment, human being.

Findley, J., "Programmed Environments for the Experimental Analysis of Human Behavior" in *Operant Behavior: Areas of Research and Application*, W. K. Honig, ed. New York: Appleton-Century-Crofts, 1966; Fig. 5, p. 838.

V-146 Relationship between selection of cigarette activity (selections/opportunity for selection) and response cost per cigarette.

Findley, J., "Programmed Environments for the Experimental Analysis of Human Behavior" in *Operant Behavior: Areas of Research and Application*, W. K. Honig, ed. New York: Appleton-Century-Crofts, 1966; Fig. 7, p. 840.

V-148 Cumulative frequency of use of the vacuum cleaner for the entire segment.

Findley, J., "Programmed Environments for the Experimental Analysis of Human Behavior" in *Operant Behavior: Areas of Research and Application*, W. K. Honig, ed. New York: Appleton-Century-Crofts, 1966; Fig. 8, p. 841.

V-149 Cumulative frequency of selection of limited toilet operations for each day of the experiment.

Findley, J., "Programmed Environments for the Experimental Analysis of Human Behavior" in *Operant Behavior: Areas of Research and Application*, W. K. Honig, ed. New York: Appleton-Century-Crofts, 1966; Fig. 11, p. 842.

INDEX